Never Surrender

A Champion's Fight

The Incredible Story of Cory Wohlford

By
Bob Davidson

Never Surrender, A Champion's Fight
Copyright © 2010 Robert Davidson

For Jon Corington Wohlford

A promise kept for Big Jon

Contents

Never Surrender

HERE I WILL FIGHT

The book you are holding is a simple tribute to an amazing man, Cory Wohlford, and his loving family. His life has been filled with incredible success on the athletic field, followed by a staggering and shocking injury that confines him every day. With the help of his family and friends, he has been able to turn his tragedy into inspiration for those who know him, hear about him, and the lucky ones who call him a friend.

Cory has a purpose for his life. He has drive, determination, and a simple understanding of God's love. Had Cory been born into a different family or didn't have the finely honed body of a superior athlete, the horrible events of July 26, 1985, would have killed him. From the time of his injury they have been there with love, dedication, and faith.

Cory has thrived, even with a disability that would completely temper most people. He has coached high school football for over twenty years, and truly made positive impacts on the lives of his players, opposing players, and the many coaches and families that are touched by the Smithville High School football team.

His parents Jon and Becky Wohlford were blessed with a spiritual life that included faith in their maker and redeemer. They needed this faith and the will to endure the personal tragedy of their promising young son and provide him the love and inspiration to become a man of faith. These are ordinary people. Our country is strong with people just like them.

Although Jon was lost to cancer a few years back, his spirit, and love still permeate the home where Cory and Becky live.

To better understand this tribute, following are Cory's own thoughts he wrote many years before we started the book.

Bright Beginning

SUCH A BRIGHT BEGINNING SO LONG AGO
MY LIFE AHEAD, SO MUCH TO GROW
A MISTAKE MADE, I CAME CLOSE TO DIE
I THINK BACK, WITH TEARS IN MY EYES

DRIVING FAST ON A DIRT ROAD,
LOOSE GRAVEL I HIT
JULY 26, 1985,
NOW IN THIS CHAIR I SIT

MY INNER STRENGTH WILL NEVER
LET ME FAIL AT THIS TASK
MY FAITH, HOPE, AND LOVE
ARE THE THINGS THAT WILL LAST

THE UPS AND DOWNS
FOR THIS POEM I WRITE
BUT DEEP DOWN INSIDE,
MY LIFE IS HERE
SO HERE I WILL FIGHT

I GRIND THROUGH
THE STRUGGLES EVERY DAY
I'LL NEVER SURRENDER,
IT'S JUST NOT MY WAY

Cory and Becky climb a mountain every day. Their journey is filled with anticipation of good things to come. She is a saint that carries on Jon's legacy of love.

The events of that summer day in 1985 are played back in the minds of those that were there nearly every day. Cory grew to accept them soon after he started his journey on wheels. He is a man of steel with a heart of gold that looks at every day as a journey to help and spread his love.

Cory has found a wonderful friend that adores him. In your reading of this book you will meet her. Their book together has yet to be written.

Enjoy the read.

Regards,
Bob Davidson

CHAPTER 1

The Grip - 1979

The sound of grunts and groans and the popping of football pads are set to a backdrop of the green grass and goal posts of a high school gridiron. A close-up of a dirty, grass stained hand with tape around the thumb is extended downward to a dirty bloody hand. The hands grip around the thumb.

Pulling back we see two strapping young men in dirty Plattsburg Tiger football uniforms, Cory and Chris Wohlford, twin brothers with the numbers 5 and 89. It is easy to see that they are the biggest and most dominating players on the field.

As Chris pulls Cory to his feet, the scoreboard in the background shows a score of Plattsburg 21 Stockton 6, midway through the fourth quarter.

"Good hit Cory!" Chris exclaims, a spitting image of his brother. As he gets to his feet Cory shouts to the rest of the defense "Five more minutes, then we are in the State Championship!"

Steam rises from the players into the cold fall air. On second down the offense runs a sweep away from Cory. From his safety position he runs across the field avoiding several blockers and makes a flying tackle for no gain.

On third and long, Cory reads a pass play, drops back into the wide open field with a receiver running toward him. The ball is in the air and just as the receiver goes up Cory delivers a devastating blow that take him and the receiver flying through the air and landing with a thud on the cold Missouri turf. Chris looks on with amazement at his brother.

"Don't think they'll try that again."

The down marker shows fourth down. Cory and Chris are in the huddle and everyone is looking to the Coach on the sideline. They can read Coach Freeman's mouth as he signals Double twist... safety blitz.

His big lineman Danny Booth sees Chris still breathing hard and says, "I'll take them outside. You get the back."

At the snap of the ball, the big tackles shoot to the outside and the defensive ends go inside. The offense has called an inside trap play. The offensive players miss their blocks because of the twisting action leaving Cory and Chris a free shot at the lonely running back. They hit him with a bone jarring tackle, taking him back several yards and planting him on his back with legs stuck up in the air. Chris reaches down to help Cory up again. The grip is around the thumb.

The referee excitedly signals first down for the Tigers as they trot back into their offensive huddle.

Cory roars "Great job. Put these guys away." Then slowly and calmly he calls the play "Broken bone right, 34 and up. Ready break!"

Booth and John Gassman lead the offensive team back to the line. They are strong and appear as fresh as the first play of the game. As the backs pass by Cory to get into their positions, he winks at his back Mike Freeman with a look of confidence, lines up behind the center, and gets the snap. Running an option to the right, he cuts up field ten yards then as he is about to be tackled he pitches the ball to Freeman who jukes and runs it to the one yard line.

The Plattsburg fans had driven four hours to get to the game and now they are going wild. Signs appear saying "St. Louis, here we come" and "State Championship." The scoreboard clock runs down showing a final score of Plattsburg 28 and Stockton 6. The Tigers started the game with a ninety-three yard kick-off return by Troy McKay and never looked back.

The team is celebrating in the middle of the field with Cory and Chris together in the center. Coach Freeman gathers the team around. Parents, players, coaches and cheerleaders all push in close to hear the hard-nosed Head Coach. This time is different. The hardness is gone from his hoarse voice as he asked the boys to drop to a knee. In the middle of the huddle he too drops to a knee, bows his head, and gives thanks for the players he is coaching. He gives thanks for the parents who have given him their trust to form their young men and he gives thanks that he is a part of such a magical season.

The stands are almost all clear. Near the top is a young blonde looking intently at the large group on the field. Having just graduated the year before, she knows all of the players and their families. She spots the two Wohlford twins on a knee near the middle of the circle. Her gloved hand reaches down and feels the silver bracelet on her wrist. She smiles.

CHAPTER 2

Plattsburg

Some might call Plattsburg, Missouri "small town America." They are right and it is something to be proud of. It is a classic small town plucked from the country music songs of today and combined with the Rockwell's of yesterday. It is a place most people can only dream about with its red brick buildings built around the county courthouse. Stately streets are lined with big oak trees. Large Victorian homes are setback from the streets in the shades of the mighty oaks. Inside those homes are families that have both parents and if they are lucky, a Grandparent or two. Front porches are for sitting and talking with the neighbors on a cool spring day, a warm summer evening, or a fall afternoon. It feels good. It feels safe. It feels like home.

This County Seat of Clinton County Missouri goes beyond the city limits signs, extending into country side down miles of linked gravel and blacktop roads. Rolling hills of lush green row crops and neatly fenced cattle ranches create vistas where one can see for miles upon miles.

Set well back from the roads are two story white clapboard farm homes or wide brick ranch style homes with gravel driveways and neatly manicured front yards. Grand oak trees frame the homes and wind breaks line the northern fence to help keep the cold winter winds from blowing through. Behind these homes are matched sheds and garages where the farmers fix the tractors and combines, plows and cultivators, balers and mowers, weld the race cars, store their tools, and gather with their neighbors to talk about the crops, cattle, or markets. Going through the gates you get to the working farm. Tall silos store the grain as they wait for the market to hit its high so they can sell. Some have a feeding operation where the corn and soybeans can be fed to the farm animals. Inside the homes are families being raised with boys and girls who are expected to pull their own weight and work on the farms. Their work is rewarding and they understand the value of the land.

Plattsburg is located directly north of Kansas City about 40 miles. If you aren't going there, the possibilities of ever knowing it exists are slim. It is not on the way to or from a city. The people of Plattsburg like it that way. They know their neighbors and look out for their own. They are all rich with the sense of community they have maintained for over 150 years.

Families have farmed the same ground for several generations. They prospered when the weather brought forth abundant crops and could make a great living when the cattle and hog markets demanded their bounty. When the crops failed or the bottom dropped out of the markets, what were once farmers and ranchers driving shiny new four wheel drive trucks are men and their families looking for ways to survive.

The city of Plattsburg dates back to before the Civil War. Its manicured tree lined streets of Victorian homes give you the feeling of stepping back into a simple time where pleasures are abundant and the County Fair is an event that everyone looks forward to from the time the last frost thaws. It is measured by the amount the local girl scouts are able to raise with their chili supper so that they could buy uniforms, or times when the whole town would be a buzz because a new Doctor's clinic is going into an old bank building. Every once in a while a scandal would break out like when the kids would white wash the streets before the homecoming football game.

Schools are top priority. Getting a good education means that you can become a productive member of the community and protect the future of this much revered small town way of life. The school is the meeting place for the community. School carnivals, dances, recitals, band concerts and sports events bring this town together. Local merchants, church pastors, farmers, and families pack the gym or football stadium. It's expected and when they don't show up, it is obvious. The community cares.

The Plattsburg rich aren't too rich and the poor aren't too poor. Those in need are taken care of by those with means. Benefactors are seldom made known and those in need are never disgraced. The town feels the pain of family hardships and celebrates the joys of success. It is evident in the way they support their teams. When the local baseball teams venture out and win a tournament it is splashed across the front page of the Clinton County Leader. Athletic stars are born into families and the old timers' recall how they stack up against their fathers and grandfathers, mothers and grandmothers. It is often said that another one of those Bennett or Harris kids are coming up to star on the football or softball team or a Norton girl is going to start on the Varsity as a freshman, just like her mom and daddy did.

Right along with the articles telling of the games is the Honor Roll. Names of students and their academic achievement are just as important in this town. Everyone has the chance to be famous in the Leader or be the center of conversation at the local restaurants.

Church is a way of life in Plattsburg. Either you go or you don't. They don't ridicule you but is it apparent that those that do attend are blessed in the community. Their work outside the walls of the churches helps preserve a way of life seldom found in a big city. By example and teaching, their community of faith reaches out to help provide the moral compass that guides the small town when the going gets tough and celebrates the achievements when victory is met.

News travels fast in Plattsburg. Everyone is connected by family or friend. People who grow up in a big city may not understand how everyone knows everyone else's business. In Plattsburg it is a matter of survival. Sure, someone may leave their door unlocked to go to the store, but it's only a few minutes away and if the German Shepherd next door doesn't scare a menace away, then the little old lady down the street or the kids riding by on their bikes might notice a strange car and within minutes the owner knows and is heading home.

If you aren't from the area or heading to Plattsburg from the surrounding ranches and farms fields, there is little chance you will turn off on one of the unmarked gravel roads that run for miles north and south out of Plattsburg. If anyone is ever passing through, they are probably taking a short cut from I-35 to US 169 to go either north to St. Joe or south to Kansas City.

When you pull into Plattsburg you know you have arrived at someplace special. Highway 116 slows as it turns the bend into the city. The Police officer is not there to stop you for speeding, unless you don't heed the 35 MPH sign that he sits behind. If you are an outsider, he knows. More important, you know he knows.

CHAPTER 3

The Cinnamon Roll Jump Shot

The basketballs are lined up on a rack at the free throw line as the bell for fourth period rings. The Plattsburg High School halls are filled with students going from class to class when the gym door swings open and in walk the Wohlford twins. They are wearing Plattsburg High sweats, having changed out of their blue jeans earlier during their lunch period.

Cory grabs a ball and flips a behind the back pass to Chris who gracefully pops a shot from the baseline. Nothing but net. The two start passing and shooting from all around the paint. They are just getting warmed up when Chris takes a dribble in the lane and slams the ball down through the rim, rattling the backboard and getting the attention of the rest of the players that have come to join them in a shoot around.

It is Monday after the State semi-final win over Stockton. Cory's hand is bandaged around his knuckles, hiding the injury that he has been nursing since the game. But this is basketball and their first game is only a week away, two days after the upcoming State Championship game next Saturday. Bruises on both of the boys' forearms are indicative of the blows they delivered in the game. But this is Basketball and they are working to get their shots back while also preparing for the most important football game their town has ever been in. *But this is Basketball.*

The twins are expected to lead their Tiger basketball team to another North Division Conference and District Championship. They wanted to take it even further and beat the South Division Conference Champion Smithville Warriors. They definitely look the part, standing tall and athletic. Both had perfected their jump shots from around the perimeter and could slam the dunk shot if the lane is open. The plywood backboard attached to the light pole in their gravel driveway had helped them sharpen their shooting skills. Those are the shots they are nailing as the rest of the team join them and start a half-court game.

Their starting guard, Troy McKay, the same senior running back that was taking hand-offs from Cory the previous Saturday, is dribbling the ball at the top of the key. He fires a pass to Cory on the wing and with one smooth motion he dribbles toward the lane where Chris has set a pick. The two boys pass each other without touching. Cory goes high into the air with a fifteen foot jump shot as Chris rolls toward the basket. In a single motion Cory knows exactly where his twin is and instead of shooting the ball he lays a perfect pass to Chris who is already airborne. As Chris catches the ball in mid-air, he is still climbing. Reaching high he is flying gracefully toward the rim switches the ball from one hand to another and then slams home a dunk that even impressed Cory.

The ball had barely gone through the rim, when there is a yell from the other end of the court.

"Coach is coming!"

McKay is able to make it around the corner of the bleachers. Chris and Cory high tail it to the bleachers and are setting on the front row bouncing the basketball back and forth when Coach comes into the gym.

All of the other non-football players are still on the court when all action stops, as the hard-nosed football coach comes walking up the court.

Looking at Cory first he says, "Aren't you the starting Quarterback for the Plattsburg Tigers and you McKay, aren't you the starting running back? How about you Mr. Wohlford?" as he looks right at Chris.

Coach warned them that they needed to focus on football until the State Championship game is over. Now he has caught them in the gym with a basketball in their hands. It was unusual for him to be back from teaching driver's education until the end of the fifth period. Now, here he is. Known as a tough coach, Jim Freeman will line up against his biggest fully padded player and without even a helmet on he will deliver a blow that will rock his world.

Coach stood for a moment with his arms crossed. Everyone in the gym teetering on what he might say next. As he walked toward Chris his voice started to rise.

"Cory, Chris, get your butt out there. Another reporter wants to talk to you."

Coach stopped before getting to the locker room. Standing right in front of him is Big Jon Wohlford. He is a taller, thicker version of the twins. They exchanged a few words.

A young reporter had been sent out from Kansas City to do a special on the Wohlford twins and their Plattsburg Tigers football team. His boss is Len Dawson, the former Kansas City Chief Hall of Fame Quarterback who had led the Chiefs to their only Super Bowl victory and had later taken over as the Sports Director at Channel 9. The reporter introduced himself as Craig Sager. Sager will leave Channel 9 in a few short years to join the team at ESPN. But now he is here to interview the twins.

The gym doors swing open as the boys walk through them side by side. Sager's eyes open wide as he stands staring at the identical twins.

Without taking his eyes off the boys, he asks "How do you tell them apart?"

Jon quipped "We don't, we just call them to the table and feed them."

"Your wife must be a great cook," says Sager.

"Her cinnamon rolls are the best and she is the one that taught them how to shoot a jump shot."

Sager introduced himself to the twins. "I'd like to interview you boys about the State Championship game next weekend in St. Louis. Can I have a few minutes of your time? We will be playing the interview at both 6 and 10 tomorrow night. Can we go out to the field for the interview?"

Just then Skip and Steve Tinnen walked down the hall. Skip is the boys' biggest fan and the Editor of the Plattsburg Leader newspaper. Steve, his son, has covered all the sporting events for the paper and the Wohlford boys had provided plenty of sports fodder and championships during the past few years.

Skip broke in just as they are heading out to the field. "Hey Craig. I'm Skip Tinnen from the local paper. If you're going to do a story on these boys, you ought to know they are better at basketball. They have also won State Championships in baseball and led the track team to the District Championship."

Coach led the group out to the field. Skip and Steve stay behind attending to other business. They will see them a few minutes later, carrying footballs, basketballs, bats, gloves, and helmets, and Steve with his much used 35mm camera.

The interview went smooth as they stood on the field in the brisk autumn chill. The boys are smart, intelligent looking and impressive. Sager and his camera crew are tearing down their equipment when Skip arrives with the gear and a big smile on his face.

"What are you pulling all that stuff out here for?" asked Jon.

"I have been waiting to do a story like this since last season," Skip says as he handed the twins the balls and gloves.

"Come on over here in front of the stands. I want to get a picture of you two" says Steve having already laid out shoulder pads and baseball gloves.

Two weeks later the Wohlford twins are smiling on the front page of the Plattsburg Leader. It is a picture that still hangs on the wall of their childhood home. Chris and Cory are standing side by side, wet with sweat from playing basketball in the gym. Chris is holding a basketball, Cory a football and both have bats. Gloves and shoulder pads are on the ground between them. If you didn't read the caption, you will never be able to tell who is who.

Jon treasured this picture the rest of his life.

A friend from their high school track team cut the article out and put it in her scrap book for safe keeping. She smiled remembering all the football and basketball games she cheered for them and the long bus rides to track meets. A twinkle in her eye and a silver bracelet hanging from her left wrist.

CHAPTER 4

Twins

Cory, Chris, and little brother Steve who is a shorter, heavier version of the twins are shooting a basketball at home. The goal is a white painted plywood backboard hung from a light pole in the gravel driveway near the large farm house. A barn with cows in the pens lies just beyond the backyard sheds. The fields slope away to woods and further beyond past the old Swan place, the banks of Smithville Lake.

Cory takes a shot from twenty foot and cleanly swishes a basket. In rhythm, Chris grabs the rebound, "Football Saturday, Basketball Monday." Keeping the rhythm Cory jumps high and putting his elbow on the rim. "State Champions on Sunday!"

Chris tosses a between the legs pass to Steve who shoots and watches the ball circle the hoop a couple of times before dropping out. They all laugh at his awkward shot. Chris retrieves the ball. "Better stick with football little brother," he kids.

Steve quickly reminds them why he was coming outside in the first place, "Mom said you have to finish feeding the calves before the pep rally."

"Did it this morning, its Cory's turn" Chris follows. Cory replies, "You didn't feed them this morning!" "No, I did," mocks Steve.

It isn't unusual for the Wohlford boys to fight like this. They are competitors and winning verbally is just as important as winning physically. Sometimes these heated exchanges get physical and today is no different, even though they are going to the State Championship football game the next day.

Chris has the ball and jumps high, cleanly shooting a twenty footer. Steve rebounds and pops in a layup. Cory and Steve fight for the ball and Steve strongly rips it away and dribbles to an open spot to shoot. He never gets the shot off as Cory tackles him from behind.

Their mother Becky, a graceful and athletic woman, comes out of the house and watches the boys wrestling for a moment, looks at her watch, then interrupts their play.

"Have you got the calves fed yet?" They stop as she ups the decibels and repeats.

Steve is now on top of Cory, "No. It's Cory's turn. We did it this morning."

Chris retrieves the ball from down the gravel driveway and makes another long shot. Before Cory can regain his balance the ball is back in Chris's hands as he follows with a slam dunk over his twin.

"Come on guys. I'll never make it to town," pleads Cory.

"Did it this morning," mocks Steve as he grabs the ball dribbles hard to the basket. He hits his mark and flies high. His big hand around the ball he palms it enough to get it over the rim. His first slam dunk.

"Did you see that?" he yells

He turns and looks, no one is looking at him, they are looking up the road.

"I did it. I dunked it!"

"Right" chuckles Chris

"You and who else?" harasses Cory

"I did, I did" he yells. But no one listens.

"No one goes to town till the calves are fed," says Becky with a lot more authority.

The car is heard coming up the gravel road toward the house. Chris looks at Cory who is smiling, as the cool breeze of a late autumn day push the clouds of dust over the corn field below revealing a shining new Camaro coming up the hill toward the stately farmhouse.

"You dog. It's Tanya in her new car. You planned this all along," claims Chris. "You are something Cory; they'll feed the calves, and give you a ride to town."

"Better than the Blue Max," says Cory. They all turn and look at a big old blue four door Chrysler sitting in the driveway.

Becky remembers all the practices and games that the Blue Max had taken them to. They had passed it down to the boys when Jon got the station wagon last year. The memories of that big old trunk stuffed with sports equipment and her big athletic husband driving with three little blonde haired boys in the back seat as the Wohlford team took to the highway, warmed her heart.

The shiny new Camaro pulls into the driveway, Journey playing loud in the eight track as two girls get out of the car.

"New car?" asks Chris

"Going to drive it to St. Louis and watch you boys win a State Championship" Tanya replies, then gives Cory a big hug feeling his muscular arms around her.

Chris turns away and shoots a sly grin to his mother, his head shaking. Steve and the other girl are shooting baskets.

"Ready to go to town for the pep rally?" asks Tanya.

Steve quickly interjects, "Gotta bottle feed the twins."

"What?" asks Tanya with a questioning look.

Chris replies, "Not us, the twin calves. The momma cow doesn't produce enough milk for two."

"We have to bottle feed them," says Cory.

Only taken back for a moment she says "Need help?"

Chris turns and winks at Cory then says "Don't know if you can handle it."

"Sure can," she retorts as Cory and Chris start walking toward the barn. Tanya comes up from behind and tucks herself under Cory's arm.

Steve is left standing alone under the basket as the other girl scurries along to catch up with them. He walks over to Becky who has both hands on her hips watching them enter the barn gate.

"Cory has more girlfriends than we have cows."

"Sure does. One day soon you'll understand," says Becky.

They watch as Cory, Chris and the girls disappear into the barn. Becky then grabs the ball from Steve and swishes a twenty-five footer. Steve retrieves the ball and turns back as Becky walks through the back door. Becky stops and turns back to Steve, "Nice dunk" smiles and goes back into the kitchen to finish kneading the dough for her next batch of cinnamon rolls for the ride to St. Louis.

CHAPTER 5

Victory Road

All across Downtown Plattsburg toward the High School Parking lot and Football field, people are busy scurrying to and from the city square. The large Victorian homes that line the street to the school are adorned with banners and signs.

Fifteen school buses are parked side by side and a large crowd is waiting to load. Cars and farm trucks are entering the parking lot. A Greyhound Bus with a Plattsburg Tigers placard pulls into the parking lot from the highway. The sight of the bus excites the crowd even more. When the bus pulls up outside the locker room, everyone sees a painted Tiger Poster has been taped over the top of the Greyhound on the side of the bus.

The High School Announcement sign reads: STATE CHAMPIONSHIP FOOTBALL GAME - ST LOUIS. Banners are flying. Excited cheerleaders, the band, students and parents are assembling to get on the school busses. Young boys are throwing a football. Another sign reads - Beat Marceline.

In a store downtown, the merchant closes the cash register, follows customers to the door, and locks it behind them flipping the OPEN sign to Closed. A sign in the window says; GO TIGERS, WIN STATE

A Statue of David Rice Atchison, the county's most historic and famous politician, stands in front of the county courthouse. He is draped in red and black streamers blowing in the wind. A sign hangs from his outstretched hand that says; GO TIGERS!!!!

Supporters' signs are in windows and front yards of every business and house. People are in a festive mood as they pack cars and trucks for the trip to St. Louis.

The Victorian lane of Eighth street leading up to the High School is designated "Victory Road." Every yard has a large sign with a

Tiger beating an opponent and the score plastered over the top. The final sign says: Undefeated and Staying that Way!

Cars are parked on both sides as the high school parking lot overflows. The townspeople walk along the sidewalks and talk of each of the victories, recalling touchdown passes, long runs, and hard hits. Everyone is dressed in red and black.

A four wheel drive truck parks on the grass. Boys wearing jeans and cowboy hats get out as another bus leaves with students singing, cheering, and dancing in the aisles. The buses are followed by a long stream of cars as a mass exodus of farmers, shop owners, gas station attendants, Nurses, Doctors and darn near every former player that ever stepped on the field at Plattsburg High School is taking the five hour trip to St. Louis in support of the Tigers.

The team is looking out of the bus windows at farm fields, brown and desolate from the recent harvest of corn and beans. Good luck signs are all along the highway. As the Smithville City Limits sign comes into view, Good Luck signs from Smithville merchants line the highway and thumbs up come from people on the streets. On Main Street horns blast as a long line of Smithville cars is prepared to roll onto the highway and follow the entourage. During the season they are enemies on the field. Now they support the pride of Northwest Missouri as they head off to do battle on the Astroturf of Busch Memorial Stadium.

The player's bus leads the caravan through Kansas City. Sitting together in their heavily decorated red and black letter jackets, Chris and Cory are looking out the window at Downtown Kansas City as they pass through, knowing that St. Louis is still hours away. The tall buildings give them a further sense of excitement before approaching Royals and Arrowhead stadiums. As the two famous stadiums appear in the window the bus slows and changes lanes to get a better view. Everyone is looking at the stadiums.

The Kansas City Royals are the pride of Missouri, with their All Stars George Brett and Frank White. The Royal Blue stadium seats face Interstate 70 giving the view of three stadium decks sitting on a perfectly manicured baseball diamond.

The Tigers and all their fans are heading to Busch stadium on the other side of the state which doubles as a baseball and football stadium for the National Football League Cardinals and Major League Baseball Cardinals. Even as they pass Arrowhead, playing in Busch is like a dream come true.

A sense of pride swells up in the small town boys from Northwest Missouri as the bus regains momentum and carries them to their first Football State Championship Title game.

"Man, are they big and beautiful?" sighs Cory.

"Yeah, do you remember telling Dad you were going to play for the Royals when we were little? Are you going to play for the Chiefs in Arrowhead too?" asks Chris.

"I just may have to," as they both laugh.

"Maybe one or the other, otherwise you wouldn't have time for the girls."

Hours pass slowly as the team sits back in their oversized bus seats and relax. The buses roll on through the cold Missouri winter afternoon. Landmarks along the way give them a sense of how far to their destination. Halfway is the bridge over the Missouri River near Columbia, home of the Mizzou Tigers. The Tigers football team is once again bowl bound and it is the topic of conversation as they rolled through town.

Passing through the suburbs, the excitement builds as they near St. Louis, driving by the legendary Lambert Airport. As the bus continues east they catch a view of Downtown. Then as if on cue, they all cry out "the Arch!!" as the prominent St. Louis icon appears on the horizon. They follow the highway and city streets with the long silver lines of the Arch directing them to Busch Stadium.

On the radio we hear the game announcers getting warmed up on the Mizzou network.

"Welcome folks to the Missouri State Championship football game at Busch Memorial Stadium in St. Louis. Is there anyone left in Plattsburg or Marceline? It looks like everyone from both towns is here as these powerhouse teams square off in the State Championship game."

The Plattsburg team is unloading from the bus where a Hotel sign says Welcome Plattsburg Tigers. Cory and Chris are looking across the street toward Busch Stadium. Dreams of future touchdowns, tackles and victory is racing through their minds. They are oblivious to radio station blasting its programming through loud speakers onto the crowded streets full of fans. All the fan and student buses get unloaded well before the team. Players, family, friends, and fans are all crowding around the player bus, getting one last chance to give the team their well wishes and encouragement.

In the radio sports booth they continue, "The tractors are parked, the shops are closed up as a whole convoy of busses and cars have descended on the city of St. Louis. Plattsburg brings in a record of 11-0 this year. They have an offense averaging thirty two points a game and a defense that has only given up thirty nine points all season. No Plattsburg team has ever gone this far. Coach Freeman is proud of a team that he calls 'Solid, Solid, Solid with every one of them being an integral part of the team.' They are led by the powerful wishbone attack with excellent line play and Cory Wohlford at Quarterback."

The Wohlford boys find their way to the stadium player's entrance. They are humbled by the sudden fame found on the street and airwaves of St. Louis. They look at each other and smile

CHAPTER 6

The Game

The Plattsburg Tigers are crowded in the locker room putting on their game face. Each player is preparing in his own way for the game. From a small radio in the corner, several of the players strain to hear what the game day announcers are saying about their team and opponent. The talk turns to the different players, each of them preparing for the game. Cory is wrapping tape around his wrist and securing the bandage on his injured hand.

Known throughout the state of Missouri is Fred White, a long time sports announcer that is handling the pregame, sending his version of the game across the state on the Mizzou Network. His voice is excited as he highlights the Plattsburg team.

"It is hard not to cite the excellent play of Cory Wohlford for his 12 tackles last Saturday against Stockton."

Players are sitting side by side on the floor with their backs against the wall, their red and black jerseys already pulled over their pads. Denny Bartee #79, Bryan Wall #26, Scott Taylor #56, Jeff Howard #59, John Gassman #67, Gailon Green #77, and Dan Booth #73 as both announcers talk of their heroics in the state semi-final game of a week ago. The Tigers are not a rah rah team. They are quietly confident in their abilities.

A toilet flushes as David Adam comes out of the bathroom. Ironically Fred is talking about how Adam had played the game the week before, while "battling the flu." He was dedicated and wasn't about to let anyone take his place. Needless to say, he had a long, lonesome ride home.

Besides Cory and Chris, the duo of Troy McKay and Mike Freeman are the playmakers for the Tigers. McKay had run back a ninety-three yard kickoff return for a score and Freeman added one hundred thirty-three yards and two touchdowns in the win. Now they lazily kicked a paper football back and forth across a table with their fingers. It loosened their tension for the moment. In less than a half hour they will take the field as the underdog team; a team that came from nowhere and now faced a powerhouse program that had dominated central Missouri for the past five years.

From the darkness of the hallway tunnel Coach Jim Freeman steps into the locker room. The team is called to huddle around him. He is a bull of a man with jet black wavy hair and his red coat stretched across his broad shoulders. His eyes are looking around at the group of players he has crafted into a successful, winning football team. All players are on a knee as he steps up on a chair and addresses them.

"Gentlemen. You have worked hard to get here." Pausing and looking around the room, he continues, "We will have to play our best game of the year to win." He stops and with a silence that speaks volumes, he looks around the locker room at everyone on the team, catching their eye only for a second or two each, but in every one of those moments, without saying a word, he gave them confidence in themselves, their team and him as a Coach.

The silence is deafening when he finally gets to Cory. From deep inside he couldn't help but smile at his field general.

After a deep breath he stepped down, bowing his head as the team said the Lord's Prayer, followed by "We ask to keep both us and our opponents free from injury. AMEN."

The boys stand and look back at their Coach. He pulls them in closer by speaking softly so everyone has to get in close to hear, and then slowly starts with, "All year long our teamwork has carried us." Building to a crescendo he builds upon each word, "Let's go out there and win—as a TEAM."

The Wohlford boys exchange looks of confidence. There is no deafening cheer, just a feeling of self-assurance and anticipation for the game. Players are slapping each other on the pads as the pregame excitement builds.

The tunnel going down to the field is dark. As the team goes out the door and down the ramp, the Wohlford boys are the last to leave.

Three brothers, poised to be on the team that carries the mantel of their town, district and region on the field.

They did not find their greatest moments on this day. It was only a block in the foundation of their lives. This foundation is so strong that it will carry a load that crumbled others.

Cory and Chris are top athletes. They are boys in men's bodies. As identical twins their blonde hair sits atop their muscular frames. Playing sports year round has finely strengthened their muscles and tuned their reaction and speed. Today they follow their team as they blast through a large paper banner onto the home field of the National Football League's St. Louis Cardinals football team. They are in a slow jog and are the last two to reach mid-field where the team is chanting and bouncing around the white helmet and red Cardinal painted on the middle of the field.

Coach Freeman enters the huddle, calming the fired up players. "This is the greatest moment of your life. Twenty and thirty years from now you will look back and remember this as one of your finest hours. Now go live it with success and use it the rest of your days. Ready....Break!"

The Tiger Captains stand at mid field with the referees. Dan Booth and Richard Wade stand across from the gold and black Marceline Tigers Captains. Plattsburg is designated the home team because of their undefeated record and margin of victory in their games. Marceline calls heads as the referee steps to the middle and flips a silver dollar in the air. Plattsburg wins the toss and elects to receive. The referee gives the final instructions to play fair and clean then as if no one else had thought about it, he says "Looks like we are in for a Tiger fight." The captains shake hands and return to their sides of the field.

Plattsburg lines up for the kick return with each player preparing themselves for the onslaught that will be running full speed trying to tackle their teammate. The Marceline kicker blasts the ball deep to the one yard line where McKay picks it up and starts up the middle.

He breaks to his left, slipping a tackle and being slowed down he is zeroed in on by three others who eventually bring him down.

In the announcer's booth Fred starts down the attributes of the Marceline Tigers and how they are a senior-laden ball club that has been building for three years toward this undefeated season.

Plattsburg lines up in the wishbone offense. Cory fakes to Adam and hands off to Freeman who sprints to the outside for no gain.

Again from the booth, "Marceline strings out Plattsburg to the sideline. They are not giving up any room in that line. Marceline brings a veteran defensive line and linebacking corps that will give Plattsburg fits all day."

Plattsburg runs the option play to the right. It is designed so when Cory gets the ball, he tucks it into the belly of Freeman. Not watching Freeman, he focuses on the line to see if there is a hole. There is nothing but a wall of Marceline Tigers. Cory pulls the ball out and continues down the line, where he is looking for the defensive end. If he sees his numbers facing him, he pitches the ball to McKay who continues to the outside for a sweep. They have it defensed perfectly and Cory is tackled for a loss. Cory makes his way back to the huddle. Not making an excuse he takes the blame on himself and looks ahead to the next play.

"Good blocks line. I just didn't get it pitched." Then he quickly calls the next play, "Roll right 86 out on two. Ready, break!"

On the snap of the ball, Cory rolls to the right and completes a down and out pass to his speedy wide receiver number eighty six Wade, short of the 1st down marker by four yards.

McKay and Mike Freeman combined for over 1,500 yards; add the 800 total yards from Quarterback Wohlford and fullback David Adam's 400 yards, and they had a backfield with over 2,700 yards between them. Coach knows they are in for a battle as their first drive netted only six yards.

Plattsburg lines up with McKay as the Punter. He calls the signals, gets the snap, and kicks a high deep punt that goes out of bounds deep in the opposing Tigers territory.

Marceline runs two line blasts in a row with Gailon Green and David Adams stopping them for short gains. On third down they run a sweep play right at Cory. After a couple of quick drop steps, Cory charges and makes the tackle, but not after the run goes for a first down.

A couple more line blasts by Marceline are stopped by John Gassman and Dan Booth. Then they go back to the outside to test Cory again. This time Cory avoids a blocker, tackling the ball carrier short of the first down.

The down marker shows fourth down. Marceline punts back to Plattsburg. McKay fair catches the ball near mid-field. The game has started like a heavy-weight fight, both teams feeling each other out. They are looking for weakness in their opponent, a position they can exploit or a definite advantage of one player over another. So far they are evenly matched.

Plattsburg takes over the ball. They are disciplined and have controlled games with their running attack. Today they will have to pull out all of their weapons and balance their plan with the passing game.

Cory is running the offense. He alternates between Freeman and McKay running the ball right and left for long and short gains. On third down he throws a down and out pattern to the left completing a first down pass to Chris as he goes out of bounds.

Cory Wohlford is on target today and showing his arm strength to the scouts in the stands. After a couple more line blasts for minimal yards, the down marker is flipped to third down. Cory rolls right and throws a deep pass down the left side of the field to Wade on a flag pattern as he steps out at the 6 yard line.

The referee signals first down. The Tigers line up, prepared to score their first touchdown of the game. Cory gets the snap from center, lets the fullback slide into the line, and hands off to McKay who follows two blockers and a strong offensive line push off the right side for a touchdown. This is Power football at its best.

As the teams line up for the conversion kick, Marceline players are still smarting about being scored on. It hadn't happened a lot against them and they are taking it personal. They are a good team and all of their starters play special teams so that they have their best players on the field at all times. The snap from center is right on target and with a quick turn Cory places the ball on the tee. Normally the kick immediately split the uprights. Not this time. Marceline put its big tackles in the middle and one of their wide receivers bounced over the top and got enough of the ball to deflect it to the left. The exact Marceline player is still unknown, and jokingly debated around the reunion tables in Plattsburg for years. The scoreboard reads Plattsburg 6 and Marceline 0 with three minutes left in the First Quarter.

The Marceline Tigers go nowhere with their next series as they run head long into a stingy Tiger defense. Plattsburg holds a narrow six point lead when they get the ball back on the punt. Two short yardage running plays picks up four yards as the fight in the trenches grows heated with Booth, Gassman, and Green pounding their opponents. Both teams have tough lines that have dominated all year. Now they are hitting equally tough players and it is taking a toll on both sides.

The yard marker flips to third down and Coach signals in a favorite play that had scored four touchdowns during the regular season. Cory fakes to Freeman into the line, rolls to the left, and fires a 21 yard bullet pass to Chris. The referee places the ball and signals a first down.

Cory leads the huddle to the line. When the First down play is snapped, he drops back and sets up, seeing a Red and Black Tiger crossing in front of the safety that is racing with him away from the middle of the field. The play is working perfect, just like Coach drew it up. The other defensive back is trying to stay with the speedy McKay as he runs straight up the field and then breaks to the outside running at an angle to the goal line out of bounds marker. Cory throws the ball high and it drops in over the top of the defensive back to where only McKay can catch it. The marker flips to first down.

Plattsburg lines up in the broken bone, flexing McKay out to the left side. Cory rolls to the left and is being chased closely by a Marceline player. He sees Chris running covered tightly on an out pattern, keeps rolling then he spots McKay racing down the sideline with a half step on his defender. He launches another high arching pass. It is a wobbly loose spiral. McKay adjusted quickly placing himself between the defensive back and the ball. Catching the ball high in the air, he takes it in for a touchdown as the defensive back lays sprawled on the field behind him, his diving attempt coming up short. McKay scores his second touchdown of the day. The team runs into the end zone to celebrate before trying the extra point conversion.

Cory is in the huddle with the team looking at him. "Good job fellas. We are going to run a fake kick roll right pass. I'll hit the out pattern." The offense is set up to kick the field goal. When the ball is snapped, Cory stands up and catches the ball, rolls right, avoiding the outside rush. He fires a quick pass, underthrowing the receiver for the first incomplete pass of the game.

The scoreboards reads: Plattsburg 12 and Marceline 0 with the clock showing less than four minutes left before halftime.

Marceline receives the kick off and work their way down field with solid running plays. Cory is lined up in his safety position as the Marceline Quarterback drops back to pass. He scans the field and sees a receiver going deep down the left side. He has the angle as he sneaks a peak over his shoulder to see if the ball is in the air. Instead the Quarterback hands the ball off on a draw play to his runningback. Cory sprints to catch him at a point just beyond the first down marker, where he thinks he has the right pursuit angle. Bam! lights out. He goes down hard on the carpet covered asphalt surface they call Astro-turf. The stars are shooting through his head. His breath is knocked out of him. He never sees the Marceline back cross the goal line or the fullback that put the big hit on him.

Lying outstretched on the field he tries hard to catch his breath but is unable. He has gotten up to his knees when Chris kneels beside him putting his hand on the back of his brother's pads.

"Just slow down Cory. Breathe slow. That guy knocked the crap out of you. Breathe slow brother."

Cory is finally able to take a deep breath and looks at Chris with a grateful smile, then rises and heads to the sideline.

"Are you OK now?" Chris asks.

"Did you get the license plate on that truck?" Cory jokes with a pained smile.

"He's OK. I'm glad he's got a hard head" Chris says to the other Tigers huddled nearby.

Marceline kicks the extra point. The scoreboard shows; Plattsburg 12 and Marceline 7 as the teams leave the field for half-time.

Coaches and trainers are tending to the usual assortment of cuts and bruises associated with hard hitting games. Coach looks at his boys from the front of the room.

"Other than that last drive, we have stopped them. Five points ain't much boys. Play as a team and never surrender!" is the only instructions he gives them before settling down with his coaches to plot the second-half strategy.

Marceline starts the second half with a short return. Their strategy is to run their best back until he breaks the game open. This chews up time on the clock and slows the Plattsburg passing game. They are successful marching down the field gaining first down after first down.

Chris is playing his best game of the year helping make a number of stops as the big Marceline running back gets behind his line and runs through the middle of the field. The ball is still far enough from the goal that the Tigers have plenty of room to give before Marceline can score. Chris knows this pattern of attack from watching the games films of Marceline all week. He was ready for the next play.

The Marceline quarterback fakes the same play into the line and then spins and hands the ball to a slot back racing to the wide side of the field. Chris sees the reverse coming and when the back tries to avoid him, he makes a bone crushing tackle.

When Chris tries to get up, he knows his ankle is badly hurt. It stuck on the carpet when the back made his cut and then rolled over on its side. Cory and Steve see the pain on Chris's face and as he stands, they put their shoulder under his arms and help him from the field.

Marceline seizes their chance to attack the outside of the weakened Tiger defensive line. They sweep the ball wide to the Plattsburg six yard line, where a host of Tigers make a touchdown saving tackle. The down marker shows a first and goal.

The Quarterback drops back on first down and tries a quick pass to the Tight End over the middle. Cory sees it coming and reaches around and breaks up the pass without touching the receiver. It is just like the drill they had done so many times in football and basketball practice.

The down marker shows second down. The Marceline Running Back blasts through the middle of the line and is stood up and tackled for a one yard gain. The ball is on the five yard line now, as the down marker shows third down.

Marceline runs an option to the right. Cory comes up strong to take on the play and turn it to the inside where the Quarterback is dropped by Gassman after a short two yard gain. The ball is on the three yard line as the down marker flips to Four.

Plattsburg must now stop the Marceline momentum. If allowed to score they will take the lead on this play. Both teams are tired from the long physical drive. Both sides are huffing and puffing. The Plattsburg players never bend over and put their hands on their knees. Coach never allows it. He has taught them to open their lungs by reaching up. The team has their back to the end zone, their arms in the air and look like they are picking cherries.

Cory tells the team in the huddle to "Be ready for an outside play."

Marceline lines up. Their big offensive linemen have looks of determination as they go down into their three point stance. When the ball is snapped they run a student body right sweep. Eight players are attacking the same point on the field at a full run. They are coming back toward Cory's side. He immediately sees the Tight End blocking down on Booth, two blockers and two backs are heading right at him. The line has it blocked perfectly and he is the only Plattsburg player that has an angle on making the tackle before they can score. He side steps one blocker, slicing between him and the other and able to set his feet right in front of the back. Then out of nowhere McKay and Gassman fly into the duo of backs knocking them both down leaving Cory to wrap up the ball carrier for no gain. The crowd goes wild cheering the goal line stand with Coach on the sideline pumping fist.

"You don't see that every day" he says to himself. Looking back at his assistant coach, "Is Chris ready to go back in?"

The assistant coach replies, "Not yet, we're taping him up now."

Grabbing Wade, Coach gives him the play. "Broken right, 27 roll 86" and sends him into the game. On the snap Cory rolls left and throws a dart to McKay on the sideline hook pattern at the twenty-five yard line.

Cory rolls left again and throws twenty yards to Wade on a drag pattern coming across the middle. He makes a diving catch with a defensive back draped on him. The ball is at the forty-eight yard line with the down marker returning to 1st down.

The gold and black defense tightens stopping Plattsburg on three straight plays. On Fourth down McKay punts the ball out of bounds deep in the Marceline territory at the sixteen yard line.

Coach again turns to the trainer, "Is Chris ready?"

"No Coach" is the reply.

Coach looks back to the field for a moment, his eyes clinch shut. Could they last much longer without Chris? Looking onto the field a feeling of infectious determination comes across his face. He knows his team will never surrender.

"OK boys, let's hold them!" he yells onto the field.

Marceline runs a series of plays that bring them near the Plattsburg end of the field. The Marceline Coaches know their big linemen are wearing the Tigers down.

The Quarterback races around the right end dodging tacklers and following his big blockers to the three yard line where Cory and McKay finally ride him down.

The scoreboard shows thirty seconds left in the third quarter and the score is still Plattsburg 12 - Marceline 7. The referee signals first and goal Marceline.

Marceline runs a power play up the middle with Gassman and Bartee throwing them back for no gain, as the quarter ends. Cory takes a deep breath then sprints to the other end of the field, ready to defend the goal. The Tigers take off after him, passing the Marceline players who are walking.

Coach quietly says to himself, "You can hold them. Believe."

The referee sets the ball on the three-yard line for the second down. Marceline runs off-tackle only to be met at the line by a hard charging David Adam, then disappearing into the middle of the Tigers pit – no gain.

The down marker shows third and goal from the three-yard line. Cory sees two wide receivers lined up on his side. He is trying to get another defensive back to come help when he realizes that Marceline has spread their offensive formation. He gets to the outside of the widest receiver who is lined up right next to the inside receiver. When the ball is snapped, he blasts the outside receiver, knocking him into the inside receiver. This action gives Cory enough time to recover and stay with the off balanced inside receiver. The Quarterback is pressured before throwing a strike to the inside receiver. When he reaches to catch the ball, Cory is able to punch it out and the pass is ruled incomplete.

It is fourth-down. Everyone in the stadium is holding their breath, wondering if Marceline will blast it through and take the lead. They confidently line up in their power formation. Plattsburg's defensive line holds and as the back tries to jump over the top of the pile, he is hit by Jeff Howard and Scott Wilson, knocking him backward into the gang of Tigers for no gain. The Plattsburg side of the stadium goes wild as they successfully defend their goal from inside the three-yard line for the second time.

With possession of the ball and their backs against the goal, Plattsburg picks up a first-down by running off tackle power plays behind those same big tackles that stopped the Marceline offense only moments before. In a short time they make it to the twenty-two yard line where on third down they come up short. A tired McKay kicks the ball off the side of his foot to the Plattsburg forty-five yard line where Marceline takes over again. Plattsburg has its back against the wall once more and time is running out. If Marceline scores they will take a one point lead and Plattsburg won't have a lot of time to come back.

Marceline sends in their big offensive linemen who have been on the bench resting during the Plattsburg drive. They fight hard for three first downs in a row. Time is running short. Cory runs across the field on every play, making a couple of tackles and insuring the backs don't cut back and make it to the end zone. Bloody knuckles stain their uniforms as the Tigers give ground to the six-yard line. Ankles, knuckles, and fingers have been taped on the sidelines. It is the end game with the State Championship on the line.

As the clock nears two minutes, Marceline is at the six-yard line with a First and goal. Cory looks to Coach on the sideline and then loudly gives the message to the team.

"This is it. We have to hold them!"

Coach is pumping his fist. "Hold them boys. Watch the sweeps!"

First-down is a run up the middle and is stopped with gang tackling at the four-yard line.

Second-down the Quarterback fakes into the line and comes around right end where Cory hits him with a ferocious tackle allowing only a yard gain to the much familiar three-yard line.

The down marker shows third-down and goal from the three. Marceline sweeps wide. Cory and Jeff Howard stop the play at the line of scrimmage as big Dan Booth puts the finishing touch on the tackle.

The down marker switches to fourth-down and goal. The clock shows less than a minute left in the game. All the time outs have been used. The moment has arrived and one of these teams will be the State Champion based on the next play.

The teams line up. The gold and black of the Marceline Tigers contrast with the red and black of Plattsburg. The late fall sun has long since set and the lights are shining off the helmets.

The stage is set when Marceline's hungry team runs to the line. On the snap of the ball they run a play action fake up the middle trying to draw the defensive backs in. Then the Quarterback rolls out to the right being chased by Bartee, every ounce of energy being exerted on this final play. From the sideline it looks like he is going to run it in for the score, but Howard has the angle on him turning him back. He sees the receiver is covered by Cory and keeps running with an eye on the goal line. McKay hems him in on the sideline. Bartee and Booth catch him as he tries to turn it up. Gassman blasts in to finish him off, short of the goal.

It is the third goal-line stand for Plattsburg this half and with less than ten seconds to go, it is enough to hold up. Plattsburg wins its first State Title.

Jubilant fans race on the field. Players, coaches, and fans are cheering. State Athletic officials make the presentation of the trophy to Coach Freeman and the team. They graciously accept the large oak trophy shaped like the state of Missouri with a bronze State Champion placard on the front. Coach raises it high as the team and fans surround him. The whole town of Plattsburg is on the field slapping backs and seeking out the heroes of the game for pictures and congratulations. They all quiet down anticipating Coach Freeman's words.

"Congratulations to our team. You worked together. We played together and today with the support of our families, friends and fans, all of Plattsburg celebrates together."

Cory with a cheerleader under each arm and Chris with a crutch under each arm come over to the end zone where their father Jon, with his large athletic build and mother Becky a graceful athletic woman are talking with younger brother Steve. Jon puts his hands out and grabs theirs with a champion's grip in a heartfelt moment of joy. Jon's eyes are red around the corners. He is proud of the effort and results of his sons in this game. His big bass voice booms out "Good job boys!" Becky with a slight chuckle is smiling broadly.

As the field begins to clear, cheerleaders climb the stairs up out of the bowl. A silver bracelet dangles on the wrist of a bright blue-eyed young blonde girl high in the stands. She catches a last glimpse at the waning celebration on the field, turns and hurries to meet her friends, a smile on her face.

CHAPTER 7

Is it Time for God and Me to Meet? - 1985

It is a late summer day of 1985 in Plattsburg. Cory is older and taller, blonde and tanned. College athletics have been good for him, filling him out with strong defined muscles and the maturity and confidence of a winner. He smoothly runs across the field to chase down a Frisbee on the fly. He has been playing Frisbee with David Gipson for the last hour or so at Perkins Park on the east side of Plattsburg. The canopy of the shade trees barely cools the heat of a summer day. The thermometer had been well over a hundred degrees for the last two weeks. The dust from the gravel roads has settled on the crops giving them a white haze. There had been no cooling rain for the last three weeks.

As Cory spins the disc back to David he asks, "What time is it?"

David looks at his watch and replies "It's after 4:00, why?"

Cory starts running toward the Blue Max. " I am going to be late. Practice for the All Star game is at 5:00, and I gotta get my stuff at home and make it to Royals stadium."

Cory slams the door of the big blue car shut and speeds off throwing gravel and dust.

Cory looks down and frowns as he realizes he needs gas. His hand slams the steering wheel. Thankfully he had picked up the mail already. The rural postal carrier had left a notice that a package needed to be picked up at the post office. Becky is expecting wallpaper samples from one of her suppliers. When he was there, he picked up the rest of the mail. He saw a letter addressed to him with a St. Louis address. He recognized the name and address of an old friend from high school. Not having the time now, he looked forward to reading her letter later.

There are only a few spots to get gas in Plattsburg so he diverts his route to Larry's One Stop. The parking lot at Larry's is a popular hang-out for the kids in the evenings. He spent time there with his high school friends after games and on slow summer nights. As he pulls in, a Farmer is fueling his tractor at the same pump. He recognizes him as a friend of the family and greets him with a smile.

"I heard you are playing at Royal's stadium this weekend," says the Farmer looking for a reply.

"Yeah, an All-Star game. Lots of scouts." he replied.

"Do the pro scouts still have their eye on you?"

"So far so good. I really need a good game tomorrow and who knows where I'll end up" says Cory.

"Good luck with that and tell your Pa and Ma Hi." as he tightened the cap on the gas tank of the old red tractor.

Cory finishes pumping the Five Dollars' worth of gas in the big blue Chrysler and runs inside to pay.

"Sorry I gotta run Bill. I got five on pump two" he says as he flattened the bill on the counter with a slap, turns, and races out the door. The tractor has pulled out of the drive onto Highway 116 and is heading in the same direction he needs to go. The engine pops and misses so the Farmer has pulled over and jumped down to see what is wrong with it. Cory pulled out and gunned the Blue Max by the old tractor, gaining speed as he waved at the Farmer in passing.

Cory is driving faster as his anxiety builds. The radio is on and he reaches to turn up the volume. Tires squeal as he turns off Highway 116 and heads south toward the old family place.

The radio announcer has come back from a commercial and starts talking about the All Star Game.

"Frank White, Royal's All Star Second Baseman is here to talk about our local baseball talent hoping to get into the big leagues. Frank sponsors a local league. Their All Star game is tomorrow prior to the Royals, Yankees game" says the announcer as he turns it over to Frank. "We are truly blessed to have the Royals support for this game. It provides a chance for the top baseball talent in the Kansas City area to showcase their abilities in front of Major League scouts" says Frank. The announcer interjects "There are a number of scouts in town besides the Royals and Yankees." "You bet there are. This talent pool has attracted scouts from throughout the league" continued Frank.

The car races around a corner throwing gravel, then crosses an old rusty iron bridge with a bridge deck made of thick wooden planks that pop as the heavy Blue Max crosses.

Cory reaches down and turns up the radio. "We are loaded with some great talent. You have to start with the Wohlford twins from Plattsburg. These tall and athletic twins are definitely top prospects. They attend William Jewell College where they not only play baseball, but Cory plays football and Chris is on the Basketball team."

"They have won championships in baseball and football and are now dealing fits to opponents at William Jewell."

The Blue Max is building speed on a black top stretch of country road. Cory has the old car floored. As the blacktop ends, gravel and dust start to fly. Cory keeps his foot to the floor as the road begins to sweep to the left. His windows are down with the hot dry wind blowing dust through the car. He looks at the clock on the dash. The steering wheel begins to feel loose in his hands. He hears the gravel hit hard against the fenders and underneath of the car with a deafening roar.

Throughout his football career Cory studied game films. He slowed them down so he could see exactly how plays were being run. Now, time slows down for Cory. Even his lightening quick reflexes are gone in this slow motion moment of his life. The popping chunks of gravel create a warning that the car is off the well-worn tire paths of the dusty road. The back of the Blue Max drifts to the right. Cory lets off the gas and steers into the skid, pulling the back right tire out of the gravel. The front right tire catches more gravel, slowing the car and pointing it in the direction of the ditch. As the skid continues he stomps the accelerator trying to right the car. Both back tires spin onto the tire paths where the gravel had been packed down into a smooth hard surface. The tires grip and he turns the steering wheel back to the left. The Blue Max didn't respond and the front tires dug deeper into the gravel slowing the front of the car. He tries to correct again when the back tires bit into the hard surface sending the Blue Max straight into the ditch at top speed. He could see the embankment coming right at him as he felt the front of the car drop into the ditch. As strong as he is the impact of the front tires dropping into the gully threw him hard toward the windshield. The grill of the car crashed into the rising bank head on. The front of the Blue Max caves in back to the engine as the windshield pops and glass flies everywhere. Cory recoiled from the initial impact as the back of the car started to cartwheel. Without his seatbelt on, he is airborne inside the car, suspended between the dashboard, ceiling, and seat. The next few seconds changed his life forever.

He felt the seat slam him like a roller coaster. It flexed under him as his weight was absorbed by the rising car. For a moment he feels like everything will be OK. He missed hitting the steering wheel when he went through the ditch and is in the middle of car when the seat catches him on the way up. He thought for a split second that he would soon be climbing out of the car and catch a ride to Royals stadium to tell his buddies about his incredible wreck.

He is still moving with the momentum of the car when his head caught the passenger head rest. His arms and legs flew up and hit the ceiling. The mail is flying all around him. It is then he is thinking of a way to tell Big Jon and Becky that the old blue car is wrecked.

The impact of his arms and legs on the ceiling is followed by the trunk of his body. The air from his lungs expelled with the thud. Cory had been hit in football, knocking the breath out of him, but this hit is a full body blow like nothing he had ever experienced.

The Blue Max is suspended in mid-air for a moment as the back continued to rise. The centrifugal force of the flipping car caught his suspended body again. He is unable to right himself in midair, his body fully extended across the top of the seatback.

The Blue Max continued its flip, gravity pulling it back to earth. The second impact started with the front of the roof crunching down under the weight of the car. He saw the crushing of the top, the crunching metal starting to flatten down toward him. His head is still on the head rest when the roof collapsed around him, the rest of his body thrown into the back seat. He immediately felt the searing pain as the twisting of his body and the impact of the roof ripped muscles and tore the nerves in his neck. The Blue Max continued to flip.

The pain is immediate, pure, and raw. He felt the nerves stretch and rip while being smashed down further into the back seat. The Blue Max hit on its wheels, the top completely level with the body. The impact is as hard as the first, but he had no breath to lose. The compartment continued to close down around him when the heavy car becomes airborne again. For an instant, the crushing and twisting stop. Then the Blue Max came roaring down on its top again with the sound of screeching metal piercing his ears.

Cory's head is on top of the broken seat, his body underneath as the heavy car slammed into the ground once more, further collapsing around him. This impact broke the vertebrae bones in his neck while the muscles tore further into his shoulders. The stretching and tearing of tissue increasing the pain like a lightning bolt.

The Blue Max lifted off its top again. This time it had been so badly crushed around him that Cory becomes one with the car and does not feel the force of the last flip until the wheels come down hard. The final slam back to earth severs his spinal cord flinging him into a space between the broken seat and floorboard, twisting his head so far to the right that his chin is behind his right shoulder blade.

Steam is rising from the engine and the radio is cracking, then everything goes silent. The Blue Max is crushed. The top is leveled with the rest of the car. The doors are crumpled and glass broken. It looks like it had been through a crusher at the junk yard. There is no sound in the field as the dust settles and the sun beats down on a hot July afternoon.

Cory tries to catch his breath. It seems like eternity as he pulls hard to try and get the oxygen into his lungs. His head is now below the broken seatback with the right side of his face against it. The left side is inches away from the floorboard. The dust and dirt are still flying and he can't see anything. Several minutes creep slowly by and he is still unable to breathe. The pain is so intense he cannot understand where he is.

In this moment he thinks "Is it time for God and me to meet?" His head twisted around, he is unable to see where he is in the car. Only with his peripheral vision is he able to see the ray of sun that snuck in between the smashed top and back door frame. The minutes feel like hours. His pain increases and only a few painful breaths come each minute. He can see the ray getting closer and tries to focus on it instead of the pain, praying for it to end. The ray illuminates his friend's letter from St. Louis as it lies on the floorboard next to him.

His mind wanders to a different time as the waves of pain increase. He remembers great times at home with his family and football games and even plays in those games. Then he starts to think of the things he regretted not doing. Deep down in his memory, he thought of his beautiful young friend from high school. They were on the track team and sat together on the bus to all of the track meets. He remembered the laughs and fun and how he and Chris had been close friends with her. He sees the letter beside him, his breath coming back in a regular but shallow rhythm.

He heard the farm tractor coming up the road and the familiar sound of the iron bridge popping under a heavy load. He is alive and fights to keep his breath. The ray, memory of a beautiful girl and the sound of the popping bridge calm him and he is able to suck in another breath, followed by another then slowly, another. He is sure that if he focuses on breathing that he will stay alive. He again prays for relief, but the searing pain continues.

It has been an hour since he saw the Farmer at Larry's One Stop. Now the tractor is heading slowly across the same iron bridge, its old engine sputtering as it slowly climbs the hill to where the land flattens out and the farm fields begin again.

Nearing the accident scene, the sound of his tractor is loud in the hot summer sun. Sitting high on the tractor seat he sees the skid marks in the gravel and the fresh dirt on the torn up road bank. When he stands up, he is able to see the crumpled Blue Max lying wasted in the field. The tractor comes to a stop and the Farmer hops off, half running up to the dusty crumpled car, stepping over the deep ruts and scars the car cut into the hard packed summer farmland. Getting closer, he slows, looking around as if not wanting to see what awaits him.

"Cory..... Cory?" he asks.

He circles the car a few times trying to see inside. Then he sees Cory's limp hand. It is the only thing visible through the crushed back window of the car. A look of fear comes across his face as tears start down his cheeks. There is no reply.

"Cory?" The Farmer puts his hands on the car as if not knowing what to do next, his head bows as he says a prayer out loud. "Lord, bless this young man and hold him softly in your hands. Please be with him. Amen."

Cory couldn't respond as he focused on the shallow breaths. The sound of the farmer's prayer is like a whisper in a stadium of screaming fans. He barely hears the prayer then felt the warmth of the sun increasing as the ray crossed the floor and touched his face.

CHAPTER 8

Paradise - 1967

There is truly a village in Missouri called Paradise. It sits on a tall ridge overlooking Smithville Lake. Paradise was there long before the lake was ever thought about. The cemetery holds the generations of families that farmed the area. Down the road and around the corner from the cemetery is the beautiful white Paradise Methodist Church. If you didn't know it had been there since the turn of the last century, you would think that it is a movie set. The ground rises from the gravel road making a yard that is big and flat enough for a baseball game and picnics.

It is evening at the Paradise Methodist Church on an early summer day of 1967. Cory and Chris are five years old and playing baseball during a picnic at the church. Cory is batting. Chris is catching with their Dad. Big Jon is going through a big wind up pitching motion. The old timers are looking on from their green lawn chairs, eating homemade ice cream and watermelon. Whack, as the ball and bat connect. Young Cory watches the ball fly away and starts running toward a paper plate first base. Chris is jumping up and down excitedly yelling

"Go Cory! Run! Go Cory!"

Cory runs toward 1st base with his father close behind, the baseball in his hand.

"I am going to beat you. You're gonna be out." the big man playfully yells in his big bass voice to his small son.

Big Jon reaches the base just after Cory crosses it. He grabs Cory in a big bear hug and sweeps him off his feet. "That was a great hit Cory."

Cory replies "I'm going to play on TV one of these days. Me and Chris are both going to play on TV." Then looking at his Dad, he says, "We really can Daddy. I know we can."

"Sure you can. Both of you can" smiled Jon.

Chris comes up from behind and catches Jon at the knees. They all drop to the ground and roll around laughing.

"You boys come on over here and eat some ice cream. You need to be strong to play on the Trimble Tigers baseball team." Becky half yells from the picnic table. The boys and their Dad are rolling around in the grass.

They stop on their elbows. Chris looks up and says "Dad, are we really going to get to play baseball on the Trimble Tigers team?" as he climbs up on his Dad's barrel chest.

"Sure, you can play for the Tigers if you do what your Momma tells you" replies Jon.

"We do Dad. We have fun with Mommy" says Cory.

Jon stands, reaches down, and grabs the boys' hands with a champion's grip, helping them up. He holds their hands for a moment looking into their eyes. Cory turns and runs to his glove. Chris runs to the ball.

Chris yells to Cory "let's play some more." Cory has his glove on and Chris picks up the ball and fires it to him.

Big Jon Wohlford is standing behind the fence of a baseball diamond seven years later. His boys are 12 years old now and on the field. Posters on the outfield wall show that they are playing for the Tri County All Stars in a State Championship Little League Game.

A catcher is squatting down behind the plate. Cory is on the pitching mound starting into his wind up.

"Come on Cory. Fire it in here" says the catcher.

Cory winds up and throws a fast ball for strike three. The team comes off the field to the cheering crowd. The scoreboard shows the game tied at 1-1 and in the bottom of the final inning.

Cory puts on his batting helmet and warms up by swinging his bat several times. When the pitcher finishes his final warm-up the catcher wings the ball to second base.

Cory and Chris are taller than the rest of the boys on the field. They are looking more athletic and smooth in their gait.

Cory gracefully strides toward the plate.   Stopping he looks back at his twin who says, "Get a hit and I'll bring you home. We'll win this in the bottom of the inning, just like the Yankees did last night."

Cory hits the first pitch to left center field, rounds first and easily slides into second base.   Players and fans are on the edge of their seats.   The crowd is cheering them on as Chris comes up to the plate. The pitcher winds up and throws a fastball for a strike.   The opposing crowd lets out a cheer of their own.   Chris digs in, scratching the dirt with his cleats.   He reaches across the plate with his bat, measuring just the right distance to get the barrel of the bat on an outside curve ball.   He takes a couple of swings and sets himself for the pitch.   The tall left handed pitcher winds up.   As he starts his delivery Chris sees his elbow lead the ball.   Big Jon had drilled them over and over on how pitches are thrown and what to look for.   Chris knows it is a curve and picked the ball up while still in the hand of the pitcher.   To him it looked like slow motion as the ball approached the plate.   He could see the spinning action with the seams of the ball rotating and causing it to start its curving trajectory. He knows the ball is heading toward the outside of the plate.   His bat flew into action arcing toward the path of the curving ball. Horsehide meets ash and the ball explodes high in the air.   The Centerfielder judges the hit, turns and runs toward the fence.   He doesn't have a chance as the ball clears the fence by several feet.

The twins meet at home plate where they jump high into air. Landing together they grab each other's hand in a champion's grip. The fans are laughing and cheering as the rest of the Tri County team joins them all exchanging pats on the back and passing along the champion's grip.

The crowd is cheering, "STATE CHAMPIONS, STATE CHAMPIONS!"

They had come a long way from playing with Big Jon at the little church in Paradise.   This is the first championship of many to come.

Each one they cherished with delight. Their appetite for championships is whet. Nothing slows them down.

CHAPTER 9

An Angel on Earth - 1985

Having just said a prayer, the Farmer is again looking into the car. He has a frightened look on his face and runs back toward his tractor as a pickup driven by a young attractive woman pulls up.

She sees the Farmer running toward his tractor as she is getting out of her truck.

"Anybody hurt?" she asks as she passes by the Farmer's tractor not taking her eyes off the smoke coming from the field. Without waiting for a reply, she runs through the ditch and up the bank toward the car. She hears the Farmer yelling as he climbs back up on his tractor.

"It's one of the Wohlford twins. I think he's dead, he's not moving" said the Farmer. He restarts the tired engine and it sputters and pops as he guns it and pulls away to go get help.

Lavonne is her name. Her family's farm is nearby. They raise cows and horses. Her passion is her horses and today she is dressed in her blue jeans and boots as she runs from the road toward the crumpled car.

All but one of the tires blew out during the flips across the field. It is hissing what little air it has left. She stops and is looking at the car when it goes totally flat, shifting the Blue Max. She is wondering if the twin is still alive inside the car and needs help. Lavonne slowly approaches the car and tries to see inside. It is smashed so bad that as she circles the car she is unable to tell if anyone is in it.

She hears the tractor slowly chugging away. Alone in the hot summer sun, Lavonne looks through a gap where the back window used to be. She is startled when she sees the limp hand. The top is crushed down so bad that she can't see any further into the car.

"Hello….. hello. Are you OK?" she repeats softly as if not wanting to know the answer. Suddenly there is a muffled murmur of pain. Lavonne races to the side of the car and finds the back door handle and bravely pulls. It doesn't move. After getting a solid grip on the door, she puts both her boots up on the side of the car and the strong farm girl pulls the door open far enough to squeeze into the small space that is left in the back seat. It is so tight that she can only push in a little at a time. She sees and feels his body now but the caved in top keeps her from moving much further in.

Cory's body is chest up but his head is twisted under him facing down. She can't see that his eyes are open but knows he is alive because of his shallow breathing. She turns her shoulders and pushes herself further into the car to see if she can help him. Getting closer she has pushed herself into a space on the floorboard between the seats. She is only inches away in the darkness. She is close enough to see his face now. Her body shutters as she is terrified by the look of pain in his eyes.

CHAPTER 10

Courtwarming - 1980

The Plattsburg gym is packed for the biggest game of the 1980 season. Smithville, an undefeated conference champion has come to play on the Tigers home court. It is Courtwarming, the basketball version of Homecoming. The Plattsburg gym is packed full of fans. Decorations and posters adorn the walls.

The Warriors boast a senior team. Cory and Chris are juniors and even at their size, it is apparent that the Warriors are much bigger. They beat Smithville's football team earlier in the school year on their way to the State Championship. A lot of these boys are on both teams and tonight, the Warriors are looking for revenge.

The teams are warming up before the game. Cory takes a jump shot from the left corner, swish. Jon and Becky are standing at the end of the bleachers. The Smithville team is running a precise warm up drill. They are well coached and their ball handling shows. Cory and Chris eye the Warriors, look at each other and crack up. They have a plan for victory and the confidence to pull it off. They love the taste of victory and beating Smithville at football and basketball in the same season will be great for the town of Plattsburg. No one recalled it having happened in the past.

Jon and Becky are talking to folks as they crowd through the doors before the game. An old friend of the family greets them and points "Hey Jon! Look at the size of that team!"

Jon replies, "They're big and tough. Most of those boys have three years varsity and they have ten seniors."

"Biggest team we have ever faced" adds another player's Mom nearby. "They can shoot too" says Becky as three Smithville players shoot long range jumpers that swish in succession. Jon follows with "They beat Platte County last week by thirty points and that was with seven players in double figures."

"We know most of their parents and the kids have been playing summer baseball together for years. Coulter and Johnston have been starters since they were freshmen" adds Becky.

Man they are really big Jon thinks to himself. The tip-off starts the game, goes to Chris, a quick pass to Cory and Plattsburg goes up by two with a twenty foot jumper. The action continues with the teams battling point for point until the middle of the second quarter. Longtime fan Dorothy Huckabee, with her distinctive voice, can be heard above the crowd. Big Jon's booming bass voice raises as he cheers the team on. The twins are scoring every other basket. The Coach calls time out to give his smaller team a rest. He knows they will have to pace the game out to keep from getting run into the ground.

Courtwarming in Plattsburg is only second to Homecoming for the biggest sporting event, dance and fun filled activities of the school year. The activities include a build-up to the big game on Friday night, followed by a dance on the gym floor where the Courtwarming Queen is crowned. The Queen Candidates sit in a cordoned off section of the gym all decked out in their beautiful dresses. Tonight, two of those Candidates, anticipate a folly from the rafters.

Earlier in the day Craig Peters and David Adam had taken two of the Candidates to the rooftop of the gym to photograph them for their inauguration pictures and the Year book layout. While they were on the roof, Craig found a trap door through the roof where he could access the rafters. He showed the two and told them he was going to toss toilet paper down during the game as a practical joke.

That night at the game Craig and David opened the trap door. They have more in mind than throwing toilet paper as Craig climbs onto the roof rafters. Without anyone noticing, he climbs across the rafters and lowers a rope at center court. The packed gym was still full because no one wanted to give up their seat. When the rope hit the floor, everyone looked up to see what was next. Craig starts to slide down the rope. It is hot and burning his hands and when he tries to re-grip, he falls even faster landing with a hard thump at half court, hitting his head. Lying on the floor half dazed, several fans run onto the court to help. All of the sudden, he jumps up and runs over to the Courtwarming Queen bows and gives her a rose as the crowd laughs and erupts into applause. This story will be laughed about at future reunions and become local legend in town. Hearing the loud laughter from the crowd, Craig Peters is propelled to become a famous comedian. There are doubts he has ever topped this stunt. Some think the head trauma is still with him.

The scoreboard shows a see saw battle with the lead changing hands. Every time Smithville goes ahead, Cory or Chris shoots and scores to put Plattsburg back on top. The Cameron radio station is carrying the game. The announcer gets so excited during the seesaw battle that he blurts out, "Somebody call the Fire Department PLEASE! Cory Wohlford is on fire tonight!"

Plattsburg starts to pull away in the third quarter. Their teamwork puts them up by eight points entering the Fourth Quarter. Smithville's Regis Coulter started the final quarter scoring by driving in for a short jumper, bringing Smithville to within six points. Cory gets the outlet pass, drives the floor, and hits a jump shot from the top of the key to answer. On the inbound pass, Chris pressures the ball and Troy McKay steals it for an easy layup putting them up by ten. The battle continues with a shootout between Coulter and Cory. At the end of the game, Plattsburg maintained its double digit lead with Coulter knocking down 14 points in the final quarter and Cory accounting for 15 points. The crowd goes wild and charges the floor. Plattsburg is on a roll.

A pretty blonde cheerleader looks down at the silver bracelet on her wrist. She flips over the loose fitting band and reads the numbers, 1979. She smiles and gives the most valuable player of the game a hug.

CHAPTER 11

Time to Start a Fight - 1985

The sun continues to beat down on the Blue Max. Grasshoppers and ants have found their way into the car. It has been half an hour since the tractor left. A couple of cars have come by, but unable to see the wreck, they pass on.

Lavonne's foot is sticking out of the wrecked car as the shadows lengthen. She has wedged her way deeper into the back seat.

"We'll get you out of here soon" she assures Cory as he groans in pain.

He is wedged down tight in the back seat floorboard with his neck at that painful angle. Her head is next to his and she is able to put her hand on his face, softly caressing his cheek. Cory thinks she must be an angel because there are no other sounds he can hear.

"My name is Lavonne. Are you Cory or Chris?" she asks. He can only gasp as his airway is still nearly blocked and his breathing labored and slow.

"You played football with my little brother. Roger Smith?" She interprets a stronger gasp as a yes. "Don`t move." Then she notices the number five on the baseball jersey he is wearing and remembers Cory's number. "You must be Cory" she says. He answers with a slight groan. All that he could muster at the moment.

Cory continues to labor with his breathing and Lavonne thinks she may hear his last breath before help arrives.

"It's not been that long" she tries to assure Cory and herself. "You were out when I first got here. They are coming. Please hold on. You have to fight" she pleads.

Cory forms the word in his mouth. Lavonne is shifting herself to ease the muscle cramps she has been enduring the last half hour. When she realizes what he is trying to say, "Dying?" She immediately says "Stay with me Cory. You are not going to die here. You can't surrender."

Lavonne hears a car coming. It skids to a stop on the road. Jon and Becky get out of the car and run up to what is left of the Blue Max.

Jon yells out in his big bass voice, "Cory, Cory!"

Becky runs full speed to the car "Cory, its Mom. We're here."

They are trying to see in the crushed car. The passenger door is smashed up. Becky tries but can't get in and can only see his legs.

Jon is able to reach over to the space that is open where the back window once was. He can't see Cory but puts his arm down through the wreckage finding and gripping his hand with a Champion's grip. There is no response from Cory's cold hand.

In a low soft voice Jon says "Cory, we're here." The reply is only a low grown. "We'll get you out. Everything will be OK."

"Baby, Cory its Mom. I love you. We'll get you out."

"It's Lavonne Smith Mr. and Mrs. Wohlford, he's not bleeding but he's been here for a long time. I think his neck is hurt real bad."

"Can you get him out?" asks Jon.

"No, he's pinned in pretty tight against the seat."

Cory takes a deep breath and with all that is in him he lets out a low grown.

"I'll get you out son. I will" Jon says as he wipes the tears away with his free hand and steels to the task.

CHAPTER 12

Homecoming - 1980

Homecoming weekend in a small town actually starts the week before. Individual classes build parade floats on top of farm trailers. The finest and newest tractors pull them through the city streets in the Friday afternoon parade. Crepe paper and paper mache mascots are being attacked by Tigers. The assembly of the floats usually takes place in a garage in town. Farm boys and city boys come together and patrol the downtown with water balloons. Freshman caught out walking in groups are sure to go home wet. Streets will be painted with Tiger paw prints leading from the edge of town all the way to the front of the school. Posters and signs call for the upcoming celebrations.

The night before the parade and game is when the bonfires are lit. Dry wood is stacked on the baseball field and fuel oil is poured on. When the fire is lit, the cheerleaders come out and perform their routines with the fire as a backdrop. The marching band comes onto the field, plays the school song, and then gets the crowd whipped up with memorable fight songs.

Tonight Coach Freeman steps out of the shadows. His hands are raised to calm the crowded stands. He has never been a man of many words. His words are chosen to inspire, to acknowledge and to praise. "This year's team is special. They have worked harder, longer and better than any I have ever coached. Tomorrow night we play Mid Buchanan, and I will tell you now…expect a victory."

The sun comes up on Friday morning. The players are wearing their game jerseys to a half day of school. Another pep rally in the gym ends before noon and the band takes its place at the head of the parade. The paw prints indicate the parade route as it winds through the town. Candy is thrown from the floats. Queen candidates ride in the back of convertibles. Boy Scouts, Girl Scouts, and 4-H Clubs march, each group happy to be with friends in the parade. They will soon have a free afternoon to hang around town in small groups with boys chasing girls and girls chasing boys. It's all in fun and what a blast it is as everyone anticipates the night's events.

The coronation of the Homecoming Queen takes place at the end of the football game. Cory and the Homecoming Queen are walking out onto the field surrounded by the Queen's Court. She is wearing the crown, holding a bouquet of roses and a football in her left arm.

The Principal steps out onto the field and says through the loud speakers, "Our Homecoming Queen tonight is Tanya Curry. Tanya is a cheerleader and plays in the band. She is escorted by Plattsburg's All State Defensive Back and Quarterback Cory Wohlford." The crowd starts cheering. Tonight is a special night for the Queen.

Tonight has also been a special night for Plattsburg football and the Wohlford boys. Cory rushes ten times for 120 yards, throws an 85 yard touchdown pass to Chris, and makes several tackles in the game. The final score is Plattsburg 40 and Mid-Buchanan 0.

Several college football scouts in their team jackets are in the crowd. The announcer finishes the festivities with, "That is twenty-four straight wins for the Plattsburg Tigers. We'll see you next week when the Tigers take on the East Buchanan Bulldogs in Gower. Coach Freeman will be facing his brother, Coach Virgil Freeman in a Halloween game that will decide the Conference Championship and a State Playoff berth. Have a good time at the dance and we'll see you next week at the game."

As the teams are leaving the field, Chris and Cory are walking with Becky and Steve toward the locker room. The William Jewell College Coaches approach them just in front of the Missouri Western State University Coaches. They are anxious to recruit the Wohlford twins. The head recruiter steps forward and extends his hand, "Cory, Chris can we have a minute with you?"

Chris chimes in "I'm Chris." Cory says "I'm Cory."

Just in time to hear Becky say, "I wonder if those numbers on your chest would have given you away."

They all laugh and the tension is broken. The Missouri Western Coaches stay back and wait in the wings.

"You played a great game tonight fellas. We think you will be great players on our team. Can you come to William Jewell for our Homecoming next Saturday?" asked the head recruiter.

"We are going up to Northwest Missouri State University next week for an official visit" replies Chris.

The second recruiter speaks up "We have another home game in two weeks. Can you come down then?"

Chris replies "Sounds good to me. Your basketball coach wants to talk and we know the baseball coach."

"Listen boys. If you want to play basketball and baseball too, we are all for it. It is not often we get athletes like you" states the head recruiter.

"Now you boys get going. There is a Homecoming Queen that has requested your presence."

"Thanks. Looking forward to it" both reply. Cory, Chris, and Becky turn and walk toward the locker room.

Jon and Steve were behind them listening. Jon steps forward, motions to the Recruiters and says "You boys better be on your best game. I went to Northwest Missouri State University and the boys really like it there. You are in luck, their Momma went to William Jewell. We're going to talk to those Missouri Western coaches next. Hope you have sharp pencils."

The head recruiter steps up "We do sir. Better than that, we have winning programs and your boys fit into our student athlete requirements."

"Good, if one of them goes, both of them go. They don't want to split up and an added bonus is this one" as he points to the growing younger brother Steve then starts to walk away.

"Count on us to keep them together" are their parting words.

Jon turns and the Missouri Western Coaches are on top of him also offering a visit.

CHAPTER 13

Brothers

Virgil Freeman had been guiding his East Buchanan Bulldogs to Conference and Division Championships until recently. His younger brother Jim had taken the reigns of the Plattsburg Tigers three years earlier and last year they were crowned State Champions. It had been two seasons since Plattsburg lost a game. This is the ultimate sibling rivalry. Tonight, the winner of these undefeated teams will play for the District crown and advance to the State Playoffs.

The East Buchanan Bulldog stadium is filling up an hour before the game. The band has finished its last preparations for the half-time show and the teams are on different ends of the field warming up. They are veteran teams and have faced each other every fall since Junior High School.

The Bulldogs stadium is built into the side of a hill. The home stands cover the hill with abundant seating and concessions. The concrete structure is one of the biggest in the conference and they have no problem packing it full of fans.

On the visitor's side are five small bleacher sets with five rows only. The Bulldogs aren't disrespectful of the visiting teams. They just allowed them to bring their own stadium with them. Several hours before the game, pickups and farm trucks start showing up. The bigger flatbeds take their position behind the bench where they are backed in to provide platforms for lawn chairs. They continue this pattern around three sides of the field with four wheel drive pickups lining each end-zone. You can step from truck to truck all the way around the field without ever going to the ground.

Farmers in their overalls, former players, and farm kids stand watching the two powerhouse programs warm up. This game is one of the most anticipated and renowned games in the history of these northwest Missouri towns which are located only ten miles apart. The attention of the state has focused on the town of Gower, home of the East Buchanan Bulldogs. Politicians are shaking hands at the gate. The concession stands open early, serving hot dogs and hamburgers. Everyone in Gower knows about the hamburgers. An anonymous farmer had donated the beef and the burgers are grilled on open flame pits. Families are lining up before the game, just to make sure they got their fill.

With less than an hour before game time the parking lots are full. A stream of cars crowd the school entrance and the locals are helping direct their opponent's fans to parking throughout the adjacent neighborhoods. State Troopers are directing traffic off US 169 Highway. The line of traffic is several miles long in both directions. As game time closes in, people park their cars on the edge of the highway and start walking toward the stadium lights.

Approaching Gower from Plattsburg, the glow of the stadium lights create a white ball sitting on the ridge at the edge of town. Above it, a full moon lights the sky creating an almost daylight visibility. Just the sight of the moon and those lights in the dark blue fall night is getting everyone excited. It's Halloween.

A TV Reporter is interviewing the Bulldogs Coach Virgil Freeman.

"Tonight your Bulldogs take on the reigning State Champion and Number One team in the state of Missouri, coached by your brother Jim Freeman. How do you counter a team that good?"

"Jim has done a great job with 24 straight wins, a State Championship and two Conference Championships" says Virgil.

The Reporter persists, "Does that intimidate your team?"

"Heck no" Virgil says looking somewhat surprised at the question.

Virgil regains his smile as the next question is raised. "The KCI-10 is one of the top conferences in the state. A victory tonight will give you a tie with your brother for the conference championship, and a state playoff berth. How do you stop them?"

Virgil confidently looks at the camera and in his best football coach voice says, "Score touchdowns. Nobody has scored on their defense this year. And we'll need to stop their quarterback. He is in Blue Chip Magazine as one of the top prospects in the Midwest. That's how we will stop them."

The reporter turns back to the camera,

"Good luck tonight Coach. It's Halloween in Gower, Missouri and anything can happen." Freeman shakes his hand, turns and runs out onto the field where his team is warming up.

The stadium is packed on the Bulldog side and the Tiger fans have filled in around the field with the first row sitting in lawn chairs, the second row standing two and three deep and behind them. Sitting and standing on the truck beds are the many family, friends, and fans that have come to watch their reigning State Champion Tigers.

A cable fence is the boundary keeping the fans off of the field. The local police department looks the other way as a group of former players and a few Dads move up and down the sideline during the game. Their sons and friends are the stars written about in the paper, highlighted on TV and radio. If Plattsburg and East Buchanan ever had star power, tonight is the biggest it has ever witnessed and the cops are not going to spoil their day in the sun.

The sideline is filled with cheerleaders and the bands are playing fight songs. The Tiger's band and most of the kids are dressed in Halloween costumes. The fall weather is crisp. The players breathe steam as they warm up.

Cory and Chris are two of the game captains leading the Plattsburg team in warm up stretching. Coach calls out loudly for his team to assemble. They come together in the middle of the field around their excited Coach. His contagious attitude is filling his team as he tells them, "Boys, this is going to be a tough game. Stop their running backs and the game will be ours." The team starts a buzz. Freeman raises his hand to quiet the excited boys. "I want hard hitting right from the start. This game could be decided by one play. Let US make that play."

The team crushes in and is now bouncing up and down. Coach Freeman yells, "Ready!" and the team yells "WIN!" They head to the sideline as the Referee calls for the captains.

At the center of the field Chris calls heads and wins the toss. The teams' line up for a hard fought football game. They battle back and forth with hard hitting, rough tackles, and all-out effort from both sides. The First, Second and Third quarters end with the scoreboard showing Plattsburg 0 and East Buchanan 0.

Kids dressed in Halloween costumes are lined up and down the fences as the Kansas City ABC TV Station camera man walks the sideline to get video of the best ones. The most popular is a Tiger with a stuffed Bulldog hanging out of its mouth. Everyone is trying to get on the news.

The scoreboard shows less than two minutes left as Cory runs an option from the fifty yard line to the twenty yard line and is tackled in bounds.

The clock continues to run toward one minute left. The down marker shows First down and ten at the twenty-yard line. Cory drops straight back, is pressured, steps up and passes to Chris who is tackled at the nine-yard line.

The clock continues to run down with less than thirty seconds left. Cory hurries the team to the line and they run an option play to the left. The running back is tackled out of bounds for no gain as the clock stops with ten seconds left.

The down marker shows third-down. Plattsburg breaks the huddle. Cory calls an audible at the line. He drops back and fires the ball to Chris in the end zone. The defensive back hits Chris before the ball gets there. There is no flag. It brings up fourth and goal for the Tigers at the Bulldogs nine yard line.

Cory calls time out with three seconds left. He trots to the sideline where Coach Freeman is grinning from ear to ear.

Coach says "Isn't this great, just like we dreamed. We are standing face to face with the one play that can win this ball game. Give me one of those great runs, son."

Before Cory returns to the huddle he looks at his Coach, mentor and friend. They had been fighting together on football Friday nights for the past four years. Cory nods and says, "I will Coach. I will."

"Blast into that end zone" is the last thing Cory heard as he confidently trotted back to the huddle.

Coach is looking at the team on the field and under his breath he says, "Cory, won't let them take him down." Next to him is his trusted Assistant Coach, Joe Trotter. Trotter hears Coach then says "I will always give it to Cory. He is a winner." Coach Freeman smiles.

The team breaks the huddle, Cory having just called the play of the game. Before getting to the line he grabs Chris and says "Let your man slip through, then go get sixty six the backside linebacker. I'm going to cut it back."

Cory lines up behind the center. "Down, Set, Hut, Hut."
The ball is snapped. Cory reaches back and bellies the ball into the right half back, flowing with him toward the line. Chris lets his man charge into the backfield where Cory would normally be, but Cory has cut hard back to his left and follows Chris back against the grain. The safety comes up strong. Chris levels the backside linebacker. Cory cuts up under the block and as the Safety flies in to make the tackle, Cory spins to the outside making him miss. The Cornerback realizes he has been suckered and breaks back toward the middle of the line only to be carried into the end zone by Cory's hard driving legs. Cory made four players miss before carrying an All-District defensive back into the end zone. Coach Freeman and Trotter are on the sideline jumping up and down, their fists in the air.

David Gipson kicks the extra point and after a hard fought second half the game ends with the scoreboard showing Plattsburg 7 and East Buchanan 0.

"And that's the game folks. Congratulations to the undefeated and un-scored upon KCI 10 conference champion Plattsburg Tigers on their 25th straight win. The Tigers advance to the State Playoffs next week against Rock Port in defense of their State Championship crown" as the announcer signs off.

CHAPTER 14

Pain - 1985

The shadows are starting to get longer. The afternoon sun has heated the field to an unbearable temperature. The dust is choking and Cory is still in the car. They are not about to move him without the paramedics. Lavonne has stayed with him. Her soothing voice and soft touch keep Cory connected. She gets more and more anxious with the anticipation and muffled footsteps outside the car.

Smithville Lake is a new lake built by the Corp of Engineers. Many of the roads that once travelled through this area had been flooded by the lake. They are now dead ends and the ambulance found a couple of them in the search for the wrecked Blue Max. As they backtracked, they too felt helpless. The dispatcher kept coming on the radio asking where they were. Trouble is, they didn't quite know themselves.

Word had gotten back to Plattsburg and several anxious townsfolk arrive at the scene and are milling about in the road with cars parked on both sides. Becky and Jon are impatiently waiting. Becky is visibly irritated. Once in a while someone will yell out they hear a siren and everyone stops, straining to hear what direction the sound is coming from.

"It has been too long Jon. Where can they be?" Becky asks

"I don't know Momma, Johnny went back and called them again. They are on their way from Smithville."

Jon's long arm is still reaching through the back window, holding Cory's hand with the champion's grip.

A car is seen screaming up the gravel road toward them. The white dust trails the car like a cloud of smoke, then settles over the line of cars that have stopped to help. All look. Jon motions with his head for Becky to come to him. She crawls up on the back of the car and reaches down through the window, taking Jon's place as he runs out to the road.

Becky yells weakly after him, "Find out what's going on Jon" as she reaches in though the back window, straining to reach her son's hand laying lifeless in the back seat. When she finally reaches it, she grasps his hand as tears roll down her cheeks. She looks down at the tear drops that have fallen on Cory's hand. Becky quickly wipes her tears before anyone sees them. Then in that voice that only mothers have, she reassures her son, "Cory, that ambulance should be here anytime Honey. I am right here."

Cory is still having a tough time breathing and the heat is making it even tougher. His mouth is dry and eyes are filled with dust. Lavonne doesn't know if he can last in the heat. She is starting to wonder about herself and is feeling fatigued as she continues to caress Cory's face.

Cory is in massive pain, his jaw is clenched tight, and eyes look helplessly at Lavonne.

Softly he says, "Out."

Lavonne musters all her strength to say "We need to stay real still until the ambulance gets here."

Cory tries to move with all his might. Lavonne feels his shoulders tighten and puts her hand on his chest.

"Cory, please honey, be still."

Cory starts to cry but is so dehydrated and dust filled that the tears never come. Becky's hand is holding his with a champion's grip. She is barely able to reach his hand and when she pulls back momentarily to adjust, she loses her grip and his hand drops. Her heart is breaking as she reaches down feeling for her son's limp hand.

"Lavonne, how is he doing?" she says down into the car, looking for any sign of hope. "I think we are losing him. We need to get him out of here fast. We are having a hard time breathing in here, it is so hot" she says. "Can he hear me?" asks Becky lying on the flattened top.

Lavonne looks into his eyes, red and swollen from the dust. She sees a slight spark of recognition, takes a deep breath "Yes, he can hear you but we are fading fast down here. Is the ambulance here yet?"

"Listen to me, both of you. The ambulance is on the way. You will be out soon. I promise."

Cory looks into Lavonne's eyes unable to focus. His eyes tell the story. He is in growing pain from the torn nerves and muscles in his neck. There is no let up as the rawness of the injury screams. The broken vertebrae, that have severed his nerves, twist and rip with every breath. Cory focuses on staying awake, afraid that his next breathe might be his last. The pain continues and reminds him he is still alive.

Minutes pass, but to Cory it feels like days. He always pushed himself just a little harder than he could bear during his athletic training. Just a little more every time he would think. Just a little more to be a champion. The pain continued to grow and he recognized that feeling of total fatigue he looked for at the end of his workouts. It is when he hit it that he knew he had given it his all.

The sun fell lower as they waited. Suddenly the crushed back seat is filled with light. A single ray, the size of a baseball bat, returned and is shooting through a small hole that had been ripped open during the wreck. It is shining on Cory's face. "I don't want to die" he thinks to himself.

Becky felt a slight movement in his hand. At first she didn't know if it is the reflexes in her hand playing tricks on her or is it Cory. Then another slight twitch.

"Cory, son I felt that. Oh baby, you hold on tight. I am here and I'll never leave you. I know it hurts, but you have to hold on. I promise you."

It is suddenly quiet around the car. There is not a sound to be heard, when from inside the car a whisper rises to Becky's ears. It is just as if a choir is singing it.

"OK Mom, I love you."

Lavonne is humming a soft tune and in that moment they all know everything is going to be OK.

The ambulance is heard in the distance. Its lazy siren seems miles away as the group stands, straining their eyes across the rolling hills to where they knew the road came out of the timber nearly two miles away. This is the route the ambulance will be taking. Suddenly, coming through the trees into the open is a red and white ambulance, its lights glaring and siren screaming. The driver is pushing the limits of the vehicle. The group watches as it nears the ninety degree turn that will mean that it is only a mile away.

Jon runs back to the crushed Blue Max yelling,

"Cory, Cory, they are almost here son. Hang in there."

The ambulance arrives and the attendants jump out and get their equipment. As they near the wrecked car one of them turns and heads back for more equipment. The attendant in charge yelled back to the returning man.

"Grab the tool box; we've got to get the front seat out.

Inside the Blue Max Lavonne stretches and kisses Cory on the cheek.

"I'm going to get out of the way. I'll be right outside waiting for you."

Lavonne slides awkwardly out of the car with tears streaming down her face. Another neighbor helps her stand up, her battered jeans and cotton top have soaked through with sweat and dirt. Someone hands her a drink and she sits down in the field waiting like everyone else.

Attendant One slides in as far as he can and starts checking Cory's vital signs.

"Where are you hurt son?"

Cory can't answer as he gasps for breath. Becky is still on top of the car reaching through the crumpled steel, holding his hand.

"His neck is hurt. He is having hard time breathing and he can't move. He is in a lot of pain."

The attendant focuses on Cory, "Let's get your vitals. Don't try to move."

The second attendant starts working loudly on getting the passenger door off and out of the way, then starts on the seat. Big Jon is helping him get it out. They see Cory's lifeless legs.

"Seat's out. We can reach him from here now."

Attendant One comes around the car with the back board. They push the board in and tape Cory to it. They are working from two different angles to quickly get Cory on the board. Attendant One has taken charge.

"We don't want to move his neck."

They twist and turn but cannot get Cory out of the confined space. Becky climbs down off the car and enters where Lavonne had been. Athletic and strong, her slender build lets her squeeze into the car. With her help they pull Cory on to the backboard and out of the car. The severity of his injury becomes apparent. His face grimaced in pain with a tight jaw. They place him on the gurney and try to roll him across the grass. It is bumpy.

Becky has gotten out of the car and come around to help get him into the ambulance. Jon and Becky are on both sides of the gurney when Cory screamed. Jon grabbed the side rail and stopped the bumpy ride, "STOP, STOP, PICK HIM UP AND CARRY HIM!" not wanting to hurt Cory any more.

Becky pleaded with the attendant "Can you give him anything for the pain?"

Several on-lookers run to help. Along with Becky and Jon, they pick up the gurney and start gingerly toward the ambulance.

The attendant responds to Becky "We can't give him anything yet. We'll have to wait till we get to the hospital."

Before they slide Cory into the ambulance, Becky is holding his hand. When they push him in, his hand lifelessly drops over the edge of the gurney. She gently places his arm under the strap and steps back, they shut the doors and the sirens start as they drive off.

Jon and Becky run to their car and gun the engine trying to catch up with the ambulance. Jon is driving right behind the ambulance.

"Was he able to grab your hand Jon?" asked Becky.

"No" his deep bass voice quivered.

"I felt him try to squeeze mine. I did Jon. He can't be paralyzed."

"He couldn't grab my hand Momma, maybe he is? Pray Momma. Pray it's not that bad" cried Jon.

"Jon, what do we do?"

"Whatever is necessary"

After a thirty-minute ride the ambulance pulls up to the Emergency Room at Liberty Hospital. The sun is setting and the lights from the ambulance are flashing through the Emergency Room door. Two nurses meet the gurney carrying Cory at the door. The attendants are updating them on his vitals. Cory is still in extreme pain, his neck at that horrible angle. They continue to wheel him toward the closed trauma area of the Emergency Room. His eyes are shut as he tries to deal with the extreme pain of the frayed raw nerves that have been torn in his spinal cord.

"Cory, Cory can you hear me?" says the Nurse in charge. Cory can only moan. "I know you are hurting. I need to check a few things."

The gurney comes to a stop in the trauma area. Another nurse joins the team. The attendants back off. "We're praying for you son. Hang in there. Don't give up" they say as they leave the trauma area.

The nurses are getting his vitals as the attendants leave and Dr. Haas enters. "I just saw his parents" as he leans over the gurney looking at the injured athlete. "Cory, it's Dr. Haas. I operated on your thumb last year."

"Miraculously he is stable, just a lot of pain, Doctor" says the Nurse in charge. Dr. Haas is gingerly moving toward Cory's head and feels around his neck, which is secured in a brace. A deepened look of concern comes across his face. The nurses take his shoes off and Dr. Haas runs his pen across the bottom of his foot.

"Do you feel this Cory?" he asks.

Cory's eyes are open and he whispers "No"

Dr. Haas proceeds, still continuing to check "What about now?"

He whispers "no" again.

Dr. Haas looks at the Nurse "Keep him immobile. We'll need some help here" and leaves the room. Coming out of the trauma room he has a worried look on his face as he walks toward Jon and Becky. He sighs deeply. "He has a severe neck injury. He might get some feeling back if the swelling goes down. We need to get him down to St. Luke's right away."

Jon immediately asks "Is it his spinal cord?"

"I am afraid so Jon. We'll do what we can, but it is in the Lords hands now."

Then he catches the Nurse "Get the Life flight pilot stat, and notify St. Luke's. I want to talk with Dr. Whitaker immediately. I am going to go get Cory ready. Come get me when you have him on the phone."

The Nurse asks "Can we give him something for the pain?" "No. Dr. Whitaker will need to examine him completely. It is too dangerous" says Dr. Haas heading back into the trauma room.

Nurse One runs toward the administration desk, leaving Jon and Becky standing. Before the Doctor enters the trauma room, he turns to Jon and Becky. "Wait here, I'll drive you." Becky looks grateful for the help. Jon says "No, we're going now and get there when he lands. Come on Momma." Jon wraps his long arm around Becky and they walk hurriedly out the door.

CHAPTER 15

Staying alive

Jon and Becky come running into the Trauma Center at St. Luke's Hospital in downtown Kansas City. The trip from Liberty to St. Luke's normally takes forty minutes. Jon drove it in less than thirty and as they pulled into the parking lot, the Life Flight helicopter had delivered Cory and is awaiting its next assignment.

"We are Cory Wohlford's parents" says Becky to the woman in scrubs standing in the hallway.

"He just arrived. Dr. Whitaker is on his way in. He is a neurosurgeon. Your son is lucky to be alive. We are going to do some testing and get him comfortable. They are x-raying him now and I'll come get you when the Doctor comes in. There is a Chapel down the hallway across from the waiting room. You'll find a phone in the waiting room. You may want to spend some time there." The look in her eyes is not encouraging. "We will do the best we can."

Jon looked at Becky, and in a moment they are walking down the hallway to the Chapel.

"Jon, this is much bigger than us. I am going to go to the chapel. Call Mom and the rest of the family. Get the boys down here. We are going to need everyone."

Jon turns into the waiting room, Becky to the Chapel.

Jon slowly dials the phone. His head is foggy as he tries to remember where Chris and Steve should be. He knows Chris was headed to Royals Stadium for the practice where he was going to meet up with Cory. He wonders where Chris is now? Jon had no idea. He can't sit down as the phone number he dialed starts to ring.

Steve answers "Wohlford residence."

"Steve this is Dad."

"Dad, what happened? People have been calling and coming by the house" Steve says, not wanting to know the answer.

"Cory is in bad shape. He had a car wreck down by the bridge" bringing Steve up to speed. "He is in bad shape Steve. I need for you to get a hold of Chris. He went to All Star practice."

"Dad, he called looking for Cory. I told him what I knew, that Cory had a bad car wreck. He is waiting for me to call back. One of his friends told him about the wreck."

"Get ahold of him and the both of you get down here to St. Luke's Hospital. It is near the Plaza" Jon slowly continues "Steve, it is not good. Get Chris down here and I'll give you the details then."

Steve answers with a short "Yes sir, will do" hangs up the phone and calls Chris who is waiting by the phone.

CHAPTER 16

Apple Butter

Like many of the families around Plattsburg the Wohlfords live in a two story farm house on a working farm. The "place" is the name that farmers in this area call their farms. Some of the "places" have been in these families for generations. The "old home place" for the Wohlford family is Becky's family farm, passed down through the family for the last one hundred years. It is called the old "Gibson Place" and is a white farmhouse that has been added on to, remodeled and updated a number of times. It still maintains its stately elegance, sitting high on a ridge overlooking the Little Platte River bottoms which is now the Smithville Lake. The huge trees in the yard create a canopy to shade the home in the summer and a wind break in the cold Missouri winters. The rolling hills of crops and woods are post card perfect every day of the year. Cory still lives there today.

The fields turn green with row crops every spring and the leaves turn gold and brown in the fall. Missouri gets four seasons and with every season change, so changes the sport in the Wohlford family, but the chores of the farm go on. The garden is planted in the spring and returns an abundance of sweet corn, tomatoes, cucumbers, beans, squash, and potatoes. Everyone in the Wohlford family has a chore. The fresh vegetables are worth the time in the garden. Keeping the "place" neatly trimmed and mowed is an ongoing task.

In the fall of 1980 the apples are especially large and juicy due to a perfect growing season. Steve has already been at Aunt Louise's house for an hour unloading bushel baskets filled with the apples. The last of the tomatoes are coming off, so the table sitting outside is full of all sizes in all stages of ripeness. They don't want the frost to get the tomatoes on the vine. Everyone fills sacks of tomatoes to take home.

As they have done for years, the annual ritual for Becky's family is to get together in the fall and make apple butter. It starts by peeling bushel baskets full of apples at Aunt Louise's house. Everyone has a favorite sharp knife, a bushel of apples, sack for peelings, a pan for the sliced fruit and a lap to do their work as they sit in a big circle. The family and friends catch up as they peel.

As the fruit starts to build in the pans, large kettles are getting hot from the fires that have been burning for the last hour. Stirring the pot is a job that requires constant attention. As the kettles start to fill up with the sliced apples, it needs constant stirring to keep from scorching or burning the apples. It takes the right balance of heat and attention to make the best apple butter in Missouri. Everyone thinks this batch has all of the award winning ingredients to be one of the best ever. It takes all of the cousins and uncles to stir the pots. There is a Texas Hold'em game going on the picnic table and the Chiefs game is on a little TV brought out and put on the end of the table where everyone can see.

Cory and Chris are fighting about who has the most hits since they started playing baseball.

"What's all this ruckus?" asks Becky

"Nothin" they both reply in unison.

"Keep stirring the pot" she instructs. "We'll have both of your rear ends if those apples stick to the side."

"Chris is the best at stirring the pot" says Cory laughing.

All morning they keep adding apples to the kettles. All morning the family team keeps the paddles going.

They talk about the lost loved ones they buried last year. The funerals are recounted and the latest updates given on those who survived.

"She is doing all right now. He had a long battle, but she was by his side the whole time" was heard about a man and wife who owned a farm outside of Paradise.

The conversation moved about a young family from Church in Smithville, "That was so sad. To lose your wife in a car wreck is horrible. To lose your wife and two children has to be unbearable"

Then they sadly remembered the young athlete from Smithville that was playing basketball for William Jewell. "Randy was doing so great. He was going to graduate last spring with a degree in accounting from William Jewell and a great basketball player. He was just about to really start his life" said Jon. Jon reflected having known his family through all the years of games. He knew and admired Randy Coulter and his father Roy. His younger brother Regis had always been a tough competitor to his boys.

"Having your door bell ring in the middle of the night and a State Trooper telling you that your son was killed in a car wreck must have been hell. That was such a sad funeral with all those young people. He was a good young man."

Becky is thinking of her own kids. Something good must surely come from this she thought as she continued to peel and say a prayer of thanksgiving under her breath.

Soon the conversation is moving to how good the crops were and that the cattle market is staying up as the sandwiches came out of the kitchen. The pots boiled, apple butter thickened and cooled, is poured into jars and sealed. The annual football game had been played in the big green yard, with Cousin Missy of course, being the only girl tough enough to play with the boys.

Life is good as the Wohlford boys left the driveway in the early evening. A special friend has come back to Plattsburg wearing a silver bracelet and they are off to see her.

CHAPTER 17

Never - 1985

Cory is laying on a gurney in the middle of the room as a portable x-ray machine is moved out of the way. His breathing is shallow and the pain has subsided as they ratcheted up the medicine in the IV. His eyes are closed as his head is being immobilized with a halo contraption. The nurse holds the sides of his head as Dr. Whitaker marks the spots where he will drill into Cory's head. The screws placed in Cory's skull will attach to the halo. He will then tighten and loosen them according to how well he heals.

They have straightened his head from the horrible angle. Even though he is sedated and full of pain medication Cory paid the heavy cost of a long journey from the wreck with nothing for the awful pain. He gritted his teeth and bore it like a true champion. This is a fight he has to win.

When Jon and Becky are finally allowed to see him, the report from the Doctor will change their lives forever. They are standing in the hallway when Dr. Whitaker stepped out of the trauma area where they have been working on Cory. He has X-rays in his hand.

"Come with me. I can explain what we are doing and his situation now." He leads them to a small waiting area and sits down with them.

"Cory is resting now. We were able to give him some morphine for the pain. He is slipping in and out. I don't need to tell you how serious the trauma is to his neck. The vertebrae were broken by the subluxation and twisting" started the Doctor.

"Is he going to be OK?" asked Becky in a soft voice, looking for some sign of optimism in his eyes.

"He is not out of the woods. The x-rays don't look good." His voice slows and he wonders how he is going to complete the next sentence. He had said a prayer over Cory and will need all the strength to even be able to tell his parents that if he survived, his athletic career is over. No pitching in the Major Leagues. The words came out like they were from another person,

"If he survives, his life will never be the same."

"Never? Oh my God. No. Can you do anything?" Jon pleaded.

Slowly Dr. Whitaker replied, "Right now we are going to try to keep him alive."

Becky and Jon sit in silence, looks of confusion and pain on their faces. They are so scared of losing Cory and now, their mind raced, not knowing what to think about the finality of Dr. Whitakers statement.

"You can go and see him soon. He is being moved into the Intensive Care Unit. It will be touch and go."

Jon's own pain is like he has never felt before. He asks, "What are his chances?"

Looking down Dr. Whitaker says "I don't know. He has been unresponsive for a couple of hours. We have him on a ventilator to help his breathing. I hope there is no brain damage, but we probably won't know for several weeks."

Becky wilts as she processes the news.

"It will be touch and go for the next week or so until he is stabilized. We just need to pray that his organs continue to work."

Becky realizes that their son will need a strong and determined Mother. She is prepared to do anything for him.

She says to Jon "You go be with him now Jon. I'll go tell Chris and Steve."

Jon and Becky stand for a moment of silence with the Doctor. Jon puts his arms around Becky and looks over her shoulder to Dr. Whitaker. "Thank you, Doctor. We know you'll do your best."

Dr. Whitaker leaves them standing, quietly holding each other. His compassion for them is apparent. He wipes his eyes.

Becky slowly walks down the hallway toward the waiting room trying to figure out what she is going to tell her other sons. She is in despair, yet she knows that she must be strong for Cory and the rest of the family. They all must go through some tough days ahead. She looks into the room through the window of the door and sees Chris and Steve half heartily watching the local sports on the TV. Both have sad looks on their face. They are sitting in chairs facing each other with the TV at the end of the room.

Becky enters the room wiping the last remaining tears from her eyes. She walks slowly over to her sons. Chris rises when he sees her and in a soft voice "Is he going to be all right?"

"Cory is fighting hard to stay alive. He has fought so hard since the wreck, just to stay alive. If it wasn't Cory, he would be dead. Right now the danger is blood clots from his injury. The Doctor said if he lives, he will never be the same."

Chris closes his eyes tight hoping this is just a dream. Steve is searching her face for answers.

"Does that mean paralyzed?" asks Chris.

Becky replies "He may never walk again."

Steve is stunned and steps back from the bad news. "If he lives? Do they think Cory will die?"

"Some Nurse came by and said the swelling may go down and.. and. We have to get another Doctor, Mom! He is wrong. I know it."

Becky's voice grows strong and she grabs Steve by the shoulders. "It is worse than we thought. Cory is fighting for his life."

"They could be wrong. Who told you that?" asks Chris.

"Dr. Whitaker, the neurosurgeon. He is the best in the city" replies Becky.

Steve and Chris step back and look at their mother for answers. Pain fills their faces. Chris softly asks "What do we do now?"

"Pray" is her faithful response. They all hug. There is strength in Becky's eyes. Chris and Steve are near sobs. Becky backs away, grabbing their hands and they start to pray.

Cory is lying flat on a bed with the halo on his head, his eyes staring at the ceiling. Nurses are finishing up tucking him in. Jon enters the room. "Cory, son, its Dad." Cory's eyes are partially glazed over. Jon approaches the bed and leans close to Cory with the sounds of the monitors in the background. Cory looks in his direction, blinking his eyes as if trying to focus. He is unable to speak, but just a wispy sound of air lets Jon know he can hear him. "The Doctor said...." Jon realizes that Cory's eyes are glazed over again. "Cory....Cory" No response. "Son, if you can hear me, I Love you and I will always be here." Jon gently puts his cheek on Cory's as his eyes fill with tears. "Get some rest. I'll be right here" promises Jon.

Cory blinks his eyes then closes them. Jon reaches over and lightly holds Cory's hand with the Champion's grip. Cory slips to sleep. "Sleep son"

Jon straightens up, looks down at his sons closed eyes, slowly releases his hand and backs into the chair next to the bed putting his head into his hands. One last time he quietly weeps for his son. It will take a team to win this one.

CHAPTER 18

Another Championship - 1984

The William Jewell Cardinals Baseball team is on the field. The scoreboards reads; Cardinals 4 Vikings 3, with two outs in the bottom of the ninth inning. Cory is throwing his warm up pitches. The ball makes a loud pop as it hits the catcher's glove. Every pitch gets harder until the last one. The Viking batter is watching from the batting circle, trying to judge the speed of the pitch and swinging at the imaginary ball. Cory's wind up is the same, the delivery is straight and true, but the ball is traveling at only half the speed. The upcoming batter twists completely around before realizing as hard as Cory throws, his change-up is what puts batters away, and he had done plenty of that this year.

The radio announcer starts "We have a close one here folks with runners on second and third base. The Cardinals bring in Cory Wohlford for the second time in this double header to put the stops to the Vikings. Wohlford got the win in the first game, coming in with no outs in the seventh and shutting the Vikings down."

The announcer continues, "Brother, Center Fielder Chris Wohlford homered in the first game and has a five RBI night going with a third inning homer and two out double here in the eighth."

Cory winds up and throws a fastball down the middle for a strike. Another gets fouled off for strike two. Cory catches the throw back from the catcher. Rubbing the ball with his back to the plate, he turns and straddles the rubber.

The announcer adds "Wohlford also plays Strong Safety for the Football Cardinals where he has three interceptions this year. He winds and pitches a fast ball that just misses the corner. Chris Wohlford also plays basketball for the Cardinals. This is one athletic family."

Cory winds up for the next pitch "Here's the pitch and Wohlford throws a change up for out number three, and with that the Cardinals take their second conference championship in a row, 4-3 here at Cardinal stadium, winning the both ends of this double-header."

The team runs to the mound and everyone is congratulating each other. After a short time they all head to the dugout. Jon is leaning over in the stands with his hand outstretched toward Cory and Chris. They reach up and grab his hand with the champion's grip as Becky stands beside them with a proud smile. They chalk up another Championship.

CHAPTER 19

Transition is Constant - 1985

Phyllis, an attractive young nurse is opening the window shades rather noisily, letting the sun shine in. Cory's eyes open and roll around trying to see. He quickly closes them and grimaces.

"Are you boys ready to wake up?" she blurts loudly. "So you are Cory, I am Phyllis. We need to check on a few things here. Is this big guy your brother?" looking down over Cory and checking his halo.

"No, I'm his Dad, Jon" Jon quickly stands when he realizes Cory's eyes are open.

"They told me I have a good looking man up here" teases Phyllis.

She goes around the bed and takes the blood pressure cuff out of the rack and puts it on Cory's arm.

"The Doctors should be here around 8:00. I am glad you're awake."

Cory's eyes open and dart around the room, he tries to move as a look of panic comes across his face as only his arms move slightly.

"Whoa partner. You had a pretty rough time of it and we don't want you to even try to move yet."

Jon slides up beside Phyllis. Cory is unable to turn and see his Dad but listens close for his voice.

"Cory, its Dad. We are at St. Luke's Hospital. We brought you down here last night in the helicopter" Jon stands tall over the bed looking down into Cory's eyes. "You have been hurt real bad son. You need to stay still right now."

Phyllis leans over from the other side so that Cory can see her. "I am here to take care of you. We're going to get you better."

Cory is now able to see her. "We are going to get real close my friend."

"When did you say the Doctors are coming in?" asks Jon. "They are getting ready now. Dad, I mean Jon, there is some coffee out at the nurse station, help yourself and take your time. I am going to wash him down real good."

Jon leaves the room as Phyllis pulls Cory's sheet back. In the waiting room Chris and Steve are laying on the couches with blankets pulled up around them. They stir as a visibly tired Jon enters the room with a cup of coffee.

"How's Cory?" asks Steve. "He finally got some rest. It's been rough. He's awake now." Chris and Steve stand up and get real close to their Dad, putting their arms around him. "When can we see him?" asks Chris. "Let's wait until after the Doctors come by this morning. They are cleaning him up now" replies Jon.

"Do you think he'll be OK once the swelling goes down?" Chris asks hopefully. Jon replies "I hope so son, but the Doctor didn't give us much hope. He said Cory's spinal cord is almost completely severed." "Is there anything they can do to fix it?" asks Chris.

"Nothing. Right now they are trying to keep him alive. He has blood clots from his injury and if they move, he'll die. They didn't give us a lot of hope boys."

Chris sits down hard, staring at nothing. Shaking his head he lowers it into his hands. He talks with his mouth between his fingers. "This can't be happening. I don't believe it." Steve looks to his father for assurance. "He is alive now. How can he just die?"

Jon anguishes "Boys, I don't know about all this stuff. Cory is in there fighting for his life. We have to be strong for him. If Cory loses hope, then he will die."

Chris clears his throat and resiliently says "He won't give up. Cory has never surrendered to anything." Looking at both Steve and Jon. "I want to go see him now!" he demands as he stands up and looks at his weary father.

"Wait a few more minutes, son. The Doctors will be in there and we can hear what they have to say."

The tension starts to subside. Then Steve remembers "There are a whole bunch of people downstairs in the waiting room. What do we tell them?" "Who is down there?" asks Jon. "His Coaches and players from his team also Coach Freeman and Coach Wallace" says Steve.

"Tell them that Cory is still alive and has the best Doctors and nurses to attend to him. Tell them that he has a serious neck injury and the Doctors hope he regains more of the feeling in his arms and legs. And ask them to please pray for Cory." Chris crosses the room and looks out the window, then turns back to his father. "I can't believe this. He is supposed to play in the All-Star game today. There are scouts here."

Jon's voice raises "Tell them all we will get back with them. You will need to go and play the game though." Chris steps forward with a demanding look. "No way, I want to see Cory. I don't give a damn about that baseball game. I just want to see Cory." Steve chimes in "Me too!" "Where is he?" says Chris as he turns and walks toward the door where Becky is just entering and grabs him. "Just wait. He is getting cleaned up. They will come get us. He is still dirty from the wreck."

Chris slumps into his mother's arms, he lowers his arms down to his sides, his mouth is held in defiance as he slowly softens and the tears slide down his cheeks. He whispers "It can't be that bad!"

"I am afraid it is. But we'll be OK" Becky assures him "Right Dad?" Becky looks to Jon who has put his arm around Steve. "Cory is strong. He is strong and you know how tough he can be." Steve turns to his Dad and Jon envelopes him in his massive arms. "If he wasn't so tough, he would be dead now."

Becky pulls Chris back to the window for a talking to. "Now you have to listen to me" she sternly says. "Cory would want you to play in the game today." His eyes well up as she looks directly into them, pleading "You need to go out and be on the field for you." Chris throws down the magazine he is holding and looks at his

Mother in disbelief. "But that doesn't matter now." "Yes it does, in more ways than you can know right now. You, me, and no Doctor can do anything for Cory right now by sitting beside his bed crying. You have to go Chris. Cory expects nothing but the best from you. The best medicine he can get now is for you to play in that game" she says. "Otherwise, this thing has beaten us all."

Chris sits down on the couch, putting his head in his hands. "I can't believe this. This can't be happening. Not to Cory." Becky sits beside him and puts her arm around his neck and kisses his cheek, "You can do it Chris."

CHAPTER 20

All Star Medicine

Royals Stadium is part of the Harry S. Truman Sport Complex. It sits down in a bowl which is clearly visible from Interstate 70 as you pull into Kansas City. Its bright blue seats perfectly contrast with the dark green field as everyone who travels the Interstate can see. It is the same stadium the boys marveled at on their way to St. Louis for the State Championship football game just a few years before. The lights are already on in the late afternoon sun.

Two teams are lined up on the First and Third baselines ready for the player introductions and national anthem.

The stadium announcer starts his welcome. "Ladies and Gentlemen, welcome to the 1985 Frank White League All Star Game at Royal's Stadium in Kansas City."

Players are shifting back and forth in anticipation of the game. A picture of Cory is projected on the Center field scoreboard.

"Before we announce the players today we have some sad news. One of our All-Stars, Cory Wohlford, was seriously injured in a car accident last night. Let's have a moment of silence for Cory." There is silence throughout the stadium as everyone has their hats off and heads bowed. He continues "We all wish Cory and his family the best in this, their time of need."

Chris is the first in line as the cameraman gets a close-up of Chris who looks tired with red eyes. The crowd is on their feet clapping. The image on the scoreboard switches to a close-up of Chris in Cory's number five jersey.

"Now announcing the All Stars. Playing Left Field, bringing a batting average of .425 is Cory Wohlford's twin brother Chris. Chris is wearing number five today in honor of his brother." The crowd continues to applaud. Chris steps out, waves softly, and looks around the stadium. He is grateful that the applause is for Cory. Putting his hands together, he bows his head slightly in thanks and steps back into line looking down to the ground.

Back at the hospital, Cory is lying flat on his back as the Doctors and nurses are adjusting the halo around his head. Blood seeps out where the screws have entered his skull. His eyes are closed as Jon turns on the radio. Becky and Steve are standing in the corner as Jon adjusts the volume. A crack of the bat is heard as he tunes in the All Star game. Everyone in the room stops and listens.

"It's a drive to right field.... They are holding Jim Coons at third as the ball comes to the infield. That's the third hit this inning and the score stands at 5-4 here in the bottom of the ninth with one out and runners on first and third. Chris Wohlford is up next."

Jon doesn't know if Cory can hear the broadcast. His eyes are closed. Jon thinks "If anyone can do it, Chris can."

"It's the fourth at bat for Wohlford today in the clean-up spot. We have been talking about Chris's twin brother and the serious car accident he was in last night. Chris told us earlier that Cory is in critical condition. He is dedicating this game to Cory. Well he is certainly playing for both of them today as he has a hit, two RBIs and scored. Chris has been hitting the ball well all season. What a fitting time for him to flex his muscles and get another hit with the game on the line."

All eyes in the room are on Cory. Phyllis is standing at the end of his bed flexing his feet back and forth. Cory's eyes are clinched shut as he envisions his brother standing at the plate facing the pitcher. The room is quiet with only the radio announcer's voice.

The announcer continues "Wohlford at the plate. Here's the pitch. A swing and a miss. Wohlford was going for the fences with that swing. The count is 0-1."

Jon tells the group "He'll lay off the next one. This is the guy Chris homered off of two weeks ago down at Northtown. He knows him well."

A snap throw to third catches the player off base and he's out. Cory's eyes flash open.

Becky notices "Look. Cory is listening. Cory, its Mom. Chris is up to bat. He is hitting for you."

Cory blinks and looks up at his Mother. Jon is now leaning over the bed where Cory can see him. "Chris will get this hit."

"Wohlford has a tall order to fill. He is facing the best relief pitcher in the league with two outs here in the bottom of the ninth. Here's the stretch, the pitch, outside, ball one" the radio blasts.

Cory's eyes dart back and forth between his mother and father as the heart monitor continues its steady beat.

Jon adds "See, Chris laid off of it. That guy throws junk when he is ahead in the count. He'll probably come back with a curve ball now. Nobody can hit a curve like Chris. What pitch did Chris homer on?"

Cory looks at his father and blinks twice.

Jon knows right away "It was a curve. You don't think he'd bring it again? Would you?"

Cory opens his eyes again and blinks.

"You are right, not in a million years" Jon smiles.

Cory stares at the ceiling as if he is looking out onto a baseball diamond. Everyone in the room has their eyes on Cory.

Cory thinks, "Chris has to know he won't. He has to!" Cory closes his eyes, his jaw set and thinks "Fast ball is my bet."

At Royals Stadium, Chris is standing at the plate taking a practice swing. He enters the box and sets for the pitch. The pitcher winds up, throws a fast ball that Chris hits to the deepest part of the outfield.

The announcer blares through the radio "Chris Wohlford got all of that one...it's to deep left field. Nelson goes up and it is out of here. Home Run! Chris Wohlford hits a walk-off home run for the win. I sure hope Cory and the rest of the family are listening. This is incredible."

Back at the hospital, Cory's eyes open, his arms raise slightly. His eyes dart around the room—to Jon, Becky, and Steve. His head won't move in the halo contraption which fits tight, holding his neck.

Phyllis is standing next to him with her hand on his shoulder "You need to stay still now."

Cory's eyes blink as he feels a deep gratitude for his brother's gallant effort.

"Well folks, Chris Wohlford did his best for his brother Cory. We'll be down on the field right after this commercial."

"He did it" yells Jon as he and Steve embrace. "He did it Momma!"

Becky is smiling in the corner. She stands and slides her way between the Doctor and Phyllis lowering her face down to Cory. "He did it for you."

Cory tries to move and shifts his weight. Becky tries to comfort him. "Chris will be here soon." Cory's eyes turn toward his Mother. Tears drip down the sides of his cheeks as Becky dabs them away. "I know. It was for you. He really did it."

The sound of the radio interrupts. "We're on the field at Royals Stadium with Chris Wohlford. That was a great hit. How does it feel to win the game like that?" Chris hesitates "It's OK. It was for Cory. It was all for Cory."

"You had a hit and two runs batted in and hit the game winning homer. What was going through your head as you were up to bat?"

Chris continues "Just focus on the ball. I was able to see it come out of his hand and it looked like a grapefruit today. I needed to hit the ball for Cory."

"You dedicated this game to Cory. Your team dedicated the game to Cory and you have come through today"

Cory is listening to the radio.

"What do you want to tell Cory?"

"I am going to tell him that I hit it as hard as I could. He's the best brother. I wasn't going to play today but Cory wanted me to play for him..." Chris is choked up. "We are a family and I will always be there for him. If you can hear me Cory, now it is time for you to show us what you are made of."

Cory searches the room with his eyes, finding the assurance of Jon, Becky, and Steve. His eyes say "I will."

"This is the best medicine for Cory. Please send our prayers and best wishes from the Royals Radio Network."

The room is completely quiet except for the low weeps of a strong family. Suddenly Phyllis breaks the tension. "I am the coach now. We are going to excuse your family so you can get a rest before that hero brother of yours gets here."

Jon stands and reaches down grabbing Cory's hand with the Champion's grip. He tries but can't squeeze his father's hand. Becky kisses him on the forehead and Steve brushes his shoulder. "Get some rest big brother."

Cory looks at his Mother as the monitors continue to beep and hiss. Becky leads Jon and Steve out the door. Steve stops and looks sadly back as the door closes.

Jon, Becky, and Steve walk wearily down the hallway. Dr. Whitaker steps out from the Nurses' station. "I was just coming to see Cory. Glad you are here. Got a moment?"

"It's been exciting in there" warns Becky. "Why, something wrong?" asks the Doctor.

"No, just listening to the All Star game he was scheduled to play in today" says Jon.

"Must have been hard to listen to?" asks Dr. Whitaker.

"No. Actually it is great for him. His twin brother Chris hit a home run in the bottom of the ninth to win the game" Jon replied

Becky piped in, "He dedicated the game to Cory. Cory's pretty worn out with everything that has happened."

"You all are so strong. It is going to take a strong team to get Cory through this. Let me tell you what we are going to do to help him mend"

A look of renewed determination comes across Jon and Becky's faces. "Just tell us what needs to happen, Doctor." He continues "Your son is in real danger of a blood clot taking his life. We need the swelling to go down and will be doing a number of tests and x-rays. Later in the week we will put him in a special bed to prevent pressure sores." Becky asks "How long before the blood clots go away?"

"I don't know about the clots." He turns as if not wanting to face them with uncertainty. "He will however be able to move his arms somewhat."

Steve speaks up "See. He's not totally paralyzed." They all agree that this is the best news they have heard.

"We will start therapy immediately to keep his muscles strong" Dr. Whitaker says

"How are we going to be able to care for him?" asks Becky.
Dr. Whitaker replies "We will teach you. He is going to need you here every day."

"Thank you Doctor. You best believe that we will take care of our boy" assures Jon

"You should probably go home get some rest and get things in order so that we can go to work here" directs the Doctor.

Jon, and Steve, arms around Becky, turn and wearily head toward the elevator as Dr. Whitaker pushes the door open to Cory's room.

Later that evening Chris, dressed in jeans and a baseball hat, comes slowly down the hallway where he is recognized by a nurse named Ginger. A look of amazement on her face she calls out to Chris.

"Chris? You're Chris, Cory's twin right?" He politely answers "Yes maam."

They stand looking at each other. Ginger, a wonderful nurse that will fast become Cory's mother hen while at St. Luke's and Chris the star of the day, his hands stuck deep in his back pockets. A somber look of loss and sadness covers his face. His eyes are weary and red with the loss of sleep and worry he has recently endured.

"Hi. I'm Ginger, Cory's nurse. It's amazing how much you look alike." Chris lights up "That's why they call us twins," as Chris attempts a smile and welcomes the conversation with her. "Well, I can see where he gets his orneriness." They turn and walk down the hall together as Chris says, "You ain't seen nothing yet. Can I see him now?"

"Just down the hall. But before you go in, can I have a minute?" she asks.

"Sure" he replies.

They stop and face each other. Ginger searches for the right words to say. Slowly and directly she looks up at the tall athletic young man and sternly brings her thoughts forth. "We have to be very careful with Cory. It is going to take time for him to heal." Chris slowly ponders what she just said then replies "We have done everything together since we were born. This shouldn't be any different."

She continues "Right now he is in serious condition and he may or may not respond to you. Don't be alarmed, it's the drugs. He has been going in and out all day and will most likely be able to hear you. He listened to your baseball game earlier."

Chris turns away, the vision of the long fly ball winning the game. He looks to the ceiling, blinks his eyes, and slowly lowers them to Ginger. "He heard it?" "Yes and it's the best medicine he could have gotten. He is so proud of you."

Chris looks appreciative at her then, "I guess that is not near as important as what you folks are doing for him." She follows with "Cory is still in real danger from the blood clots. If he survives…"

Chris cuts her short and with a stern voice he proclaims "He will survive. I am his brother and his best friend. Where we come from, you don't turn your back on either. Can I see him now?" he demands.

Pausing for a moment, they both realize they are on the same team and only want the best for Cory. She grabs Chris's hand.

"I'm proud to meet you Chris and yes, he is in the second room on the left. You are good medicine."

Chris shakes her hand and gives her a hug, then turns and walks toward the room. He looks back with a determined smile on his face as he pushes open the door. Ginger feels his brotherly love.

The
Wohlford
Twins

Perfect form

Cory, Steve and Chris

Big Jon and his boys

Becky and her boys at Plattsburg High School Mother's Night

Big Jon's favorite picture of the twins

Cory and Chris receive District Championship Trophy as
Steve looks on.

Cory turns the corner in the Missouri State Championship Game 1979

Plattsburg High School,
Undefeated Missouri State Champions 1979

Cory knocks one out at Kansas City Royals Stadium
(now Kauffman Stadium)

Cory played for the William Jewell Cardinals two weeks after thumb surgery - 1984

Cory and Chris before 1984 Frank White All-Star Game at Royals Stadium

The Wohlford Family just two weeks before the accident

Cory with the halo screwed into his head on the rotating bed

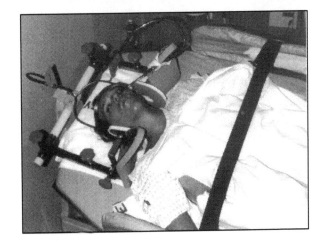

William Jewell College Graduation 1987

Head Coach Vic Wallace (by Cory) and the William Jewell College Football Coaching staff

Head Coach Bill Maas (middle back) and the Smithville High School Coaching Staff of 1991

Cory sits on his sideline perch and confers with long-time friend Denney Fales and Warrior Player Jimmy Odneal

Chris and Cory before the Brother versus Brother game of 1991

Cory's biggest fan Becky and littlest fan Peyton Wohlford (Chris's Daughter)

Brenda Norton with Cory. A dream and prayer come true.

CHAPTER 21

The Shotgun

Chris is driving the Blue Max, his girlfriend Linda sitting between the twins. They are on their way to pick up a blind date for Cory.

"You are going to like Debbie. She is real pretty" says Linda.

Cory is leaning back, soaking in the description of his blind date. Chris adds "Tall, brunette and athletic."

A smile comes across his face and he looks up trying to imagine what she might look like from the description. Farm fields are flying past as the big blue car heads down the two lane highway. This sounds good to Cory. He is always up for meeting beautiful girls.

"You guys want to have some fun?" Linda says with a mischievous look on her face as they pass a tractor pulling a load of hay and heading in the same direction. "Instead of Cory going to the door, why don't you go, Chris?"

Chris states "Like we have never done that before."

"What?" she asks.

"Was it Chris you went to the movies with last week?" asks Cory.

"I'm not worried about the movies, it was afterwards" she teases. They all laugh as the Blue Max pulls into the country lane that leads up to a picturesque ranch home set back on the ridge of a gently sloping field of fresh cut hay.

Confidently she says "You guys are too funny. I can tell the difference."

Chris pulls the car up the white gravel drive to the house. He gets out and goes to the door. Before ringing the bell he looks back with a mischievous look on his face. Debbie's father, a big farmer dressed in work pants and a hunting shirt, opens the door and Chris enters.

"We won't tell her till we get to the One Stop in Smithville" says Linda as she and Cory jump in the back seat.

"She'll probably never want to go out with me again" Cory replies.

"Think again. I know her and she is not going to give up a chance to go out with the most adorable quarterback in the state" Linda says.

Chris and Debbie come out the front door followed by her Dad who is shining the barrel of a new Ducks Unlimited Shotgun. He watches them while shining the metal. Chris opens the door for Debbie and they climb in.

"Hey Linda, Chris. Sorry about my Dad Cory" says Debbie.

Chris, who Debbie thinks is Cory, says "He's not over protective is he?"

"He just won the shotgun in a Ducks Unlimited Raffle. He wanted to show it to me. Nice guy" defends Chris.

"He thought you were nice" says Debbie

Linda leans forward on the front seat quickly changing the subject she says "I have been dying to see Raiders of the Lost Ark. Everybody is talking about it."

Cory says "It's supposed to be full of action. Lots of action. Harrison Ford is really good?"

Chris turns the car around and asks "Who's Harrison Ford?"

The car pulls out of the driveway and heads down the road.

"How do they tell you two apart?" asks Debbie.

Linda says "There is a secret. Just call their name and the right one will look."

Debbie quickly says "Cory!"

Chris is on to her and answers "Yes."

Cory tunes in and in the same voice says "Yes."

"You guys are too funny."

As they head through Smithville toward Kansas City, Chris pulls into the One Stop. Linda turns around and winks at Debbie. "Gotcha, this is Cory and he is Chris." "Stop it. No really, who is who?" asks

Debbie. "I'm sorry, they made me do it" pleads Chris. They are all laughing as they get out of the car.

"So you're Cory?" asks Debbie. Linda grabs Chris by the hand and gives him a big hug and kiss.

"That's right. It is nice to finally meet you."

"You guys are mean" she laughs.

Chris pipes in "Just remember, blue shirt. It's his favorite color and the color Mom has been dressing him in since we were little."

Linda looks puzzled. "Wait a minute. You were wearing a blue shirt last weekend Chris."

Chris avoids the observation and laughs "I'm going to get a Coke. Would you like a Coke?"

Linda nods as a couple friends, Rhonda and Shonda twin blondes pull into the parking spot beside them. Cory and Chris greet the attractive twin girls with big hugs. They are longtime friends from Plattsburg. They are all laughing as Cory retells the story, his date Debbie wondering what she has gotten herself into. Cory asks the striking twin girls "You two haven't ever done anything like that, have you?" In unison they reply as if on cue "No, No, we wouldn't ever do anything like that." Their contagious laughs taking over as they exchange mischievous looks. "Besides, I like athletic guys and Shonda likes tall guys" says Rhonda. In an ornery tone that gets him a sharp look from Linda, Chris quips "Sounds like we might be in luck." Rhonda fires back "No way, you guys are like brothers to us...No way." The brothers feign a sulk and both say "Shucks" as they leave the four girls chattering in the parking lot and enter the front door of the convenience store to get their soda pops.

Once inside they go directly to the Men's Room. Chris looks at Cory "Switch?" "Switch" he confirms.

They trade shirts and head out the door laughing.

CHAPTER 22

Without Words - 1985

Chris comes in the hospital room with a wide grin on his face. He slowly approaches the bed. Cory's eyes are closed and the monitors continue their constant beeping. "Cory? Cory, are you awake?" he slowly asks. Cory's eyes don't open as the lonely monitors beeps are the only sound in the room. "I wish you were out on the field with me." Cory can hear Chris as he lay in a drug induced state. He thinks to himself. "I was Chris. I saw the whole thing. You knocked the snot out of that ball."

Phyllis enters the room with another nurse. "He has been asleep for about an hour" she says. Chris leans curiously over Cory, looking at the device screwed into his skull. He turns to Phyllis. "Is this the Halo?" "Yes. It immobilizes his neck."

Chris gets closer and looks at the bolts in Cory's head. "But it's screwed into his head." Chris straightens up and turns to Phyllis with a serious look. "Are the blood clots better?" "No. We'll keep him on IVs and keep his legs warm while monitoring his heart and lungs. That's what those pesky monitors are doing."

Chris looks at the variety of machines surrounding the bed and hooked up to Cory. "Does he really need all these machines?" "It is a precaution. We'll probably have them off in a couple of days." Chris stares down at Cory with a concerned look. "Just keep talking to him" she says.

"It was a long hit. I knew it was out. I wish you had been there to see it."

Cory's eyes stay shut, but he still hears. He wishes he could speak, but try as he may, he cannot. He thinks "I was right there. I saw the whole thing through the radio. I saw your warm up swings, and your swing for the fence."

Chris continues "It was like you were right there telling me what he was going to throw."

A moment of silence as Chris searches for words. Cory tries to open his eyes, but the drugs are too strong.

"We are going to get through this right?" thinks Cory.

"Mom and Dad, me and Steve, we are all going to be here for you. We're going to get you healed up and get you home real soon" says Chris. Being identical twins they have never had to speak much to communicate so Chris knows Cory hears and understands him.

"It's going to be different, a lot different now" Chris reassures him. "You are on a winning team. We will always be winners."

"But what am I going to do? I can't play baseball or football and I won't be able to coach. And what girl is going to want me now?" thinks Cory as he starts to feel his own pity. Chris dismisses even thinking about what won't happen. He is happy his brother is alive. "We need to work as a team. Remember when we won the state championship in football? We did it as a team and we'll do this as a team also. Now you have to focus on getting better. You have always been a fighter and always a winner. Not everyone knows how to win. You do and you will keep on winning Cory. Keep on winning."

Cory tries to speak and signal that he understands what Chris is saying. After many attempts he quits in frustration, and thinks "I'm glad you're here."

"I will always be here. Always. You just keep showing us the way to win." Chris grabs Cory's hand and softly holds it with the Champion's grip. "Thanks my brother." Cory finally relaxes and stops fighting the drugs.

Chris reaches up and turns off the main lights in the room. Several hours pass and Cory opens his eyes to a room where the monitor lights reflect off the shiny metal and hard corners. He hears the sleeping sounds of Chris who is stirring in the chair next to his bed. He looks at the ceiling and can make out the square tiles with the little holes and crevices filled by the darkness of the room. Outside the door he hears the ongoing restlessness of activity by the nurses as they attend to others in the late evening. He closes his eyes and there is nothing there.

The dull pain has been decreasing since the nurse had given him the shot yesterday, or was that the day before. Suddenly a sharp pain begins again at the base of his neck. His face grimaces as the pain increases. He winces as the pain spreads into his shoulders and up his neck. His eyes search frantically for a sign of anyone in his room. He is unable to speak. Moving his lips he is unable to make the smallest of sounds. Chris stirs in his light sleep. "Wake up Chris. I need help" he thinks. Within seconds and without words Chris is awake.

"Uh...What?" Chris stands and turns on the light above his bed. Cory's eyes are open. Chris can see the pain in his eyes and Cory still can't speak and thinks "I hurt real bad."

Chris asks "You want me to get a nurse?" He blinks twice and his eyes settle as he feels the strength of his twin in Chris's eyes. The pain begins to subside just because Chris is there.

"No. It'll be OK. I just needed to know you were here" thinks Cory.

"Let me get something for your pain. No need to try and be a hero."

Cory blinks as if to say OK but he wants to scream out "I can't feel nothing and can't move nothing." Chris sees the helpless look come over Cory and gets real close, face to face. "It's just like basketball. If you can't drive, shoot the jumper. You can't let it beat you. You are the toughest guy I have ever known. Never surrender."

Cory acknowledges. The fight ahead will be like nothing he has ever trained for. "It is just so hard" he thinks.

Chris leaves the room and returns shortly. Cory can see the top of the door, but can't tell who came in until his tall, strapping brother is nearly over him. "The Nurse is coming with a shot." A new night nurse comes in and puts a shot in his IV. Cory slowly drifts to sleep. His last thoughts are "I have to figure out what I am going to do?"

The Doctors want Cory to heal his torn muscles and bring the swelling around his spinal cord down. They don't want him to even try to move so they keep him heavily sedated for nearly a week. While he comes and goes, he is never fully awake and talking. The whole community, his school friends and fans, his team mates, coaches and opponents and even strangers that are in prayer groups throughout the city await the results. They have been told he has some paralysis and they also know that he is still in danger for his life. Everyone prays for him.

As a week passes, the nurses and therapists have Cory moving with caution every day. Today a therapist is putting Cory through therapy. They have to keep his muscles limber, especially while he is on the drugs they have to move all his muscle groups. He feels what is going on, but is still foggy from the drugs. He is tired as the nurses stretch him out and massage his muscles in the rotating bed. It was a good workout he thinks as he drifts off to sleep.

CHAPTER 23

The Dream in the Crowd

The dark halls of the hospital are quiet now as the long hours of the night shift quietly pass. It has been nearly a week since the wreck. To Cory it has been a lifetime. Time has slowed down with the realization that things have changed. No matter how hard charging and packed full his life was, now it is different. The slower pace is not like him. Everything he did was always at light speed.

The drugs are working, at least the pain drugs and those other drugs that kept him in a daze so he won't try to start moving too soon.

As the night goes on, Cory is dreaming. It is a clear beautiful sun shining day. He is standing next to a local TV Reporter who is interviewing him. Cory's football team is warming up behind them. He looks around at the immense bowl of Arrowhead stadium. He is finally coaching in the big game.

"Going into the season there were those who suggested that someone should hide the helmets or sabotage the bus so your team won't have to endure a season of misery" stated the Reporter.

"Yeah. We read those stories too."

"You started out the season losing every other game. That had to be hard to keep fighting back after those losses. Yet you endured to beat some of the strongest opponents on your schedule."

Cory shakes his head "Every team we faced was a strong team and every week we got better, we got stronger, and we gained confidence." He is shifting back and forth, his hands deep in his back pockets. He easily fields the questions with a confident smile.

"What your team did is amazing, blasting through the district playoffs never allowing a point to be scored against five top ranked teams."

"We are proud of our defense."

The offensive team is warming up their passing game behind the interview. A receiver catches a pass and makes a cut before reaching them.

"Your offense, during that run of victories, scored an average of over 30 points per game."

Cory looks at Arrowhead Stadium as fans are streaming in.

"We have one more game tonight. Marceline is the Number One ranked team in the state and we are here to finish this out."

"When you were a player at Plattsburg High School, you also faced Marceline in the State Championship game and won. You weren't picked to win that game either, what about tonight?" asks the Reporter.

"I tell my kids the same thing that my Coach, Jim Freeman, told us back then. 'Play as a team and you'll win as a team' Never Surrender"

"Those are words to live by. It's a beautiful night here in Arrowhead Stadium and it looks like the whole city has come out to this championship game. You have quite a following of supporters" admires the Reporter.

"Yes we do"

He wishes Cory good luck then throws the interview back to the booth.

Cory turns toward large groups of fans that have pushed their way to the front row seats and are hanging over the edge. As he trots up to the group they are yelling support. He reaches up and grabs a hand out of the crowd. It is hard to make out the face of the attractive young blonde woman. They grip with the Champion's grip, only this time he places a kiss on the outstretched hand with the dangling silver bracelet. To cheers from the crowd he turns and runs to the tunnel and his waiting team.

"If they win here tonight with a shutout, they will be the first team to win the State Championship by holding all of their playoff opponents scoreless" starts the TV announcer.

In the locker room the team is huddled around Cory. He stands tall in the middle. "Men, you have made me and our town proud. It has been a long and tough road. Now we have one more game to prove ourselves. If we go out and play as a team....we will win as a team!"

The team gathers closer as they put hands high in the air, grab the guy in front of them, and yell "TEAM!"

Cory raises his hand for one last word before leading the team onto the field. "This is your moment. Seize the moment and go get your Championship."

The tunnel out to the field at Arrowhead is large enough to drive a tractor trailer truck through. Both teams are in the tunnel waiting to be announced on the field. Cory instructs his team to keep their eyes forward as their opponents line up beside them. He wants them to focus on the task at hand and not be distracted. He leads the team onto the field, letting them pass him as they break through the paper sign. He is the last one through the sign as he walks up to number Five, his starting quarterback.

Cory holds his gaze on his field general.

"You must lead the team while you are on the field. The rest of the team will follow you and how you play. It takes a team to win. I know you can do it."

After a quick smile he walks toward the sideline, his eyes searching the crowd. He finally finds an arm waving back and forth and a large smile breaks over his face. He is unable to clearly see the face of the young blonde. A reflection of the stadium lights glisten off of the bracelet on her wrist.

His team receives the kick-off. They slug it out with numerous hard hitting plays. The dream is vivid. His quarterback throws long and short, runs inside and out, but neither team is able to score. It's as if Cory is playing every position on the field. He throws, runs, tackles and is in on every play. He is also on the sideline calling every play. He has to use all of his football skills in this game. There is no let up. The dream doesn't slow down as the clock runs.

His dream continues after halftime with more action on the field as the teams counter each other in a game of strategy. Cory knows that one wrong move—a blown coverage or an interception—can ruin their chance at success. In the fourth quarter Marceline kicks a long field goal to go up by three.

Cory's team finds their back against the wall late in the game with only thirty seconds left and down by three. The ball is on their one yard line and it appears Marceline is ready to score the knockout punch. They have played their butts off against a good opponent, an opponent that is undefeated and top ranked team in the state. Now they needed their coach more than ever.

Cory calls a timeout. The team is huddled around him. He is smiling with an excited look of anticipation on his face. The boys are spent and some look ready to give up.

"Gentlemen, we will not surrender now. We can stop them and get the ball back. We can score, this is football and this is life. We can win this game. This is what you live for. This is why you trusted me to lead you when you walked on the field for that first hot August practice. Nobody said this would be easy. Finish strong now and you will always know how to win."

He smiles with an air of confidence. Looking around the group his gaze stops for a moment with each boy to instill the confidence just as Coach Freeman did so many years before. He is amazed and proud of his team and they know it.

"We are going to stop them. Seven man front. Linemen are the plows, shoot across low and fast. You backs hit the holes between the guards and over the tackles. Go over the top. Do it and we will get the ball back."

Then he laid out the strategy for final success after goal line stand. "When the referee places the ball, be ready and get lined up quick. Run the shotgun option right before they have time to react. With no time-outs we have to score on one play. Never Surrender boys. Ready 1-2-3 and they yell TEAM!!!" as Cory releases his pumped up team with their orders.

The team runs onto the field. Just as planned, the linemen plow through, pushing the offense back. The big runningback doesn't have a chance as five defensive players meet him at the line of scrimmage and turn him back stopping the Marceline Tigers short of the goal. With the ball ending up six inches from the line, the scoreboard clock shows twenty seconds left in the game.

The TV announcer yells out, "That was an incredible goal line stand! But unless they make a big play here, Marceline will end up as the champion."

Just like they were instructed, the offense lines up immediately after the referee sets the ball. On the snap the quarterback shuffles down the line. On the fifth step he has to decide whether to keep it, turn up field and outrace the other team to the goal or pitch it. Marceline's defensive end makes the decision for him. The quarterback sees his jersey numbers meaning that he is positioning to tackle him, so he pitches the ball. The pitch is perfect traveling the short distance end for end and floating right in front of the tailback. The excited back momentarily takes his eye off the ball, distracted by an onrushing linebacker. The ball hits the ground in the end zone, Cory's heart sinks, but only for a moment. In his rush to retrieve the ball the tailback kicks it toward the sideline. The oblong ball bounces every direction before bouncing right up to him as a Marceline player dives in to recover. He dodges the player and cuts back making another miss with his unexpected move. He quickly picks up a block from the Tight End which springs him out of the end zone. Heading toward the middle of the field other players lay down pancake blocks, paving the way out to the twenty where he cuts back to the outside and picks up a wide receiver as they pass Cory running up the sideline. He throws his headset off as he cheers on his runner. The back cuts back at mid-field behind the block of his wide receiver. Cory stops and watches as his team celebrates in the end zone. State Champions....again!

The TV announcers are nearly hysterical as they yell into their microphones "They have done it, the complete Cinderella story.

Coach Wohlford has led his team to a win on the last play of the game. There is magic in the air."

There is a camera in Cory's face with the reporter sticking the mike close as Cory turns from a group of celebrating players. The reporter grabs him by the shoulder,

"That was unbelievable. What did you tell your players?"

"Simple, Never Surrender. There was still time on the clock and they needed to play this game to the end."

A short blonde comes up beside Cory and buries her head in his shoulder with a huge hug. Her face is turned away but her bracelet shines in the light.

The Reporter continues "Did you ever in your wildest dreams think your team could score with only 20 seconds and running the ball out of your own end zone."

Cory confidently replied "Yes...Yes. Anything is possible." He turns and hugs the blonde. The camera holds on them as he starts to stir from his dream, their image is flashed onto the huge scoreboard TV screens. He smiles.

CHAPTER 24

Bad News

Cory is lying tilted up sideways in the rotating bed. His eyes are closed. Jon and Becky stand near the foot of his bed. Coach Freeman is standing next to them. "He gets better every day" says Becky. They talk about the blood clots and how it seems like the last week has been an eternity. The clots have not dissolved so Cory is still not out of the woods. Coach Freemans says "Everyone in Plattsburg and Smithville and all the other towns around have been praying for both Cory and your family. There are articles in the newspapers and stories on TV."

They knew about Cory's friends staying at the hospital, keeping a vigil and saying prayers in the chapel. "Every time we go down to get a bite to eat, someone is there asking about him" says Jon. "I saw several people from up home when we came in. They want you to know they support Cory and you guys too."

Becky walks to the head of his bed and lightly touches his face. "He knows how to beat this. He is so strong Coach." Becky smiles her way through the tough moments, not showing her emotions often, but now she starts to tear up and Coach Freeman hugs her close comforting her. Jon stands and walks across the room.

"Most important is the blood clots haven't worsened." Coach Freeman turns to Cory and gets real close so Cory will hear him. "It's not over yet. Fight for it Cory. You always find a way to win. This battle will go on and on and you have to fight for it every day."

The bed continues to roll to the side. A tear starts on the inside of Cory's eye and rolls across his lashes toward the ground. The bed is nearly perpendicular now. Coach Freeman notices the tear right before Cory coughs to clear his throat. He looks at Becky.

"Do you see that?" Cory hasn't been able to speak but a few words since the accident. He clears his throat again and says,

"Mom."

Becky gets down on a knee so he can see her. "I'm right here."

"Mom, I'm sorry."

Jon pushes the call button for the nurse.

"You don't need to be sorry baby. It's not your fault."

Phyllis immediately appears and takes control of the room. "Did you have a nice rest young man? You have been out of it for a week. Again, I am Phyllis, your new Coach. Can I get you something?"

Cory asks for a drink and Phyllis pours it and puts the straw in his mouth. He slowly takes a long drink as everyone in the room looks around gratefully. Big Jon's wide smile shares the relief they all feel.

"Jim, tell them downstairs that Cory is better. They are waiting for any good news" says Jon.

"My pleasure" Coach Freeman grabs his jacket, says goodbye with hugs. He lightly touches Cory's shoulder then says a quick goodbye and leaves.

As Jim Freeman, the tough Coach of Plattsburg is walking down the hallway he is wiping the tears from his eyes. He pushes the button for the elevator just as it starts to open. Chris and Steve step off and greet their former Coach. He is so emotional his voice cracks and all he can say is, "He's awake."

Chris yells "Great!" and sprints down the hallway not looking back until he is walking into Cory's room.

"He just woke up" Coach adds with a big smile.

Steve follows Chris turning and backpedaling as he watches Coach Freeman get onto the elevator. A quick wave and before he is gone Steve echoes a half dozen thanks down the hall.

Back in the room Chris comes in the door. Cory's bed is turned awkwardly up on its side. Chris immediately drops down on his knees so that Cory can see him. They both smile.

"You're late!" Cory says. "Where have you been?" replies Chris. Cory tells them about his dream "It was so real, like a dream but so real. I know I can handle this now Chris. I am mad as hell about it, but I can handle it."

"You bet we can" says Chris.

Jon stands up from the chair and grabs Chris around the neck and says "Absolutely. Thank God."

Steve comes in the door and sees Cory awake. He can hardly speak as he looks at his big brother on the bed. "Everyone has been praying Cory. People have stayed down in the chapel all week. There must be thirty people down there tonight."

Dr. Whitaker pushes the door open and steps into the room. "Good, I am glad you are all here."

Steve and Chris are hoping the doctor is going to tell them that the swelling is starting to go down and that Cory will be walking out of the hospital soon. The anticipation rises as the Doctor comes to the edge of Cory's bed. He reaches down and grabs Cory's hand.

"You are quite a young man. That is why what I am about to tell you is so tough," he swallows hard. "We have been working hard to keep you alive and keep your spirits up. It looks like the clots are dissolving and you are getting better."

"Well, that's good news, right Doctor?" Jon asks

"That is not the only news I am here to tell you" he slowly starts. "We have looked at everything and I am afraid, Cory," he pauses "you will never be able to walk again."

Cory looks from the Doctor to Big Jon who is stunned at the finality of the statement. Big Jon summons only one word, "Never?"

"I am truly sorry. I wish there was something more I could do or say, but the injury has caused permanent damage."

Cory feels as if the breath has been knocked out of him again. The pain he sees in his family's eyes is too much for him. As if on cue, Phyllis comes in and pulls Cory up into her arms to hold and assure him.

"It is going to be OK Cory. We are all here for you. Soon you'll be able to go to a hospital that specializes in your type of injury and they will really put you through the paces."

She continues to hold him and looks at the sad eyes of his family. The Doctor's head is bowed as he lifts Cory's hand with the Champion's grip.

"All the changes that are happening to you have happened to others. Your challenge is to overcome them and make a life for yourself. Can you do that Cory?" asks Doctor Whitaker.

Cory is stunned. Phyllis has leaned him forward in the bed and is holding him up.

"I think I can," he says, still trying to process the news. He looks at the Doctor, "Never?"

Doctor Whitaker shakes his head and continues.

"I would like you to go to Craig Hospital in Colorado for therapy. They will teach you and your family how to live with this. They are very good."

"Then that is what we will do" Jon says strongly. "We are going to get you better and get you home."

Doctor Whitaker gives them a few more details and tells them he will arrange for Cory to go to Craig, says "Goodbye" and leaves.

Phyllis doesn't let a moment go by that she isn't trying to move things forward. She lowers Cory and tells him to get ready. They have some work to do to get him ready for the trip. The family is stunned and everyone is processing the news in their own way. Cory knows he must show his courage now.

"I want to tell everyone downstairs thanks for their prayers."
Becky stands up and walks toward the door. "I will do just that. I am going down to talk to some folks now and get a Sprite."

"Better tell them from now on, I will be the short good looking twin," jokes Cory. They all laugh trying to break the tension. He smiles although inside he is crying out in pain. Not so much for him, because he knows he can get through anything, but for his family and the uncertainty that had been caused. The look on their faces pains him greatly.

CHAPTER 25

The Pink Letter

Cory is lying on a bed with a rack of pulleys and weights above him. His halo is prominent as a therapist is helping him adjust and move his arms up and down against the weights. They talk about how he used to train with weights and he jokes about being able to lift the whole bed before his accident.

The walls are covered with cards. There is so many that some are the same, only the well-wisher is different. His favorites are the ones from the kids at church. They made them with macaroni and all kinds of buttons last week during Bible School. He smiled and laughed when Becky brought in a whole grocery sack of the cards. She showed him each one as they try to figure out who each kid is and their parents. Most of the kid's parents, brothers and sisters, grandparents and great-grandparents were long term members at the Church. They recalled the births, marriages, and funerals of those families during the long hours in the hospital.

Cory laughs when Becky comes in this morning carrying another sack of what they now affectionately called macaroni cards from the Baptist Church Bible School. They looked at each one and laugh at the pictures knowing that each one took a long time to make and a lot of love is felt. Cory is starting to hold them now and as he lies flat in the bed, he can hold them for a few seconds after Becky reads them to him. He admires the cards and has her tape them on the wall. The walls in his room are nearly covered. He jokes that they will never need to buy macaroni again.

Becky carries another sack into the room with cards that had been mailed. She lifts it to show Cory. He is still getting twenty to thirty cards and letters a day. Becky opens each one, reads it, and then shows it to Cory, holding it just far enough from his head that he could see it. They save the funny ones for Phyllis so they can all laugh. He even got a few risqué ones from his team mates and Becky show those to him anyway.

Today is a little different. After they read all of the cards and letters, Becky gets real quiet. She is holding a letter on pink stationary next to her heart. Phyllis is adjusting Cory in the bed and washing him from top to bottom.

Phyllis has Cory dried and the sheets changed. They are bantering over the Royals and Red Sox game from the night before. George Brett had a double to win the game in the ninth inning. Cory tells her that the Red Sox pitcher should have never thrown a curve ball to Brett.

"He is the best curve ball hitter in the league and maybe the best ever. I think he will be a Hall of Famer" says Cory.

Phyllis disagrees. As they banter back and forth, Becky sits and holds the pretty pink letter, looking at it and not quite knowing how to bring it up with Cory.

"Phyllis, can you help me with this? I have read so many letters to him this morning but this is a special one" says Becky.

She stands up where Cory can see her. As she looks down on him, a large muscular man lying in the bed, she wonders how she will ever be able to handle him like Phyllis and the other girls on the floor of the hospital.

"You got a really nice letter from someone today. I didn't quite know how to take it. I think you need to hear it though. It came from someone who knows what you are going through."

Phyllis opens the pretty pink envelope and pulls the letter out and begins to read.

"Dear Cory.....

My name is Cheryl Green. My sister-in-law Paula goes to your church. She told me about your accident and asked me to write to you.

In March of 1978, I was in a car accident which broke my neck and injured my spinal cord. I was 24 years old. My husband and I had only been married 2 1/2 years. I can still remember the fear and confusion. How could God allow something like this to happen to me? I was angry and bitter and so afraid. Believe me I know and understand what you are going through right now. I can only encourage you that it will get better.

These first months are your most difficult. There are people who care about you and are praying for your recovery. Most important, God cares. He loves you and will give you the strength to get through this. Lean on him!

It's OK to allow yourself to express what you are feeling though. Don't think you have to be brave or strong. If you feel angry and frustrated, it's OK. If you feel depressed and want to cry, then cry. You need to be able to get those feelings out. Believe me, it's better than trying to hold it all inside.

Cry out to God. Tell him how you feel. He does hear you. The nights are always a hard time for me. So lonely and it is hard to fall asleep. All you can do is just lay there and think. I learned to pray and talk to God at night.

Having lived through it, I understand that you may feel hopeless and so full of despair, but there really is life after paralysis. Remember; 'He is near to the broken hearted and the crushed in spirit.'

With Jesus Love,
Cheryl Green"

Phyllis finishes the letter and with a look of stern support she says, "I can help you heal your body, stretch your muscles and teach you how to work a wheel chair, but this is about what is truly important. Your soul."

Then she places the pretty pink letter over his heart and smiles.

CHAPTER 26

Friends

When young friends face a critical injury like Cory's, they begin to take stock of themselves as if "What would I do if it happened to me." They are concerned for their injured friend while at the same time it gives them a dose of reality that they too could end up in the same situation.

Life had been good for Cory. He enjoyed the fame of a super star athlete and stayed humble. He was nice to everyone and knew the younger kids were looking at him as a role model. All throughout his career at Plattsburg and at William Jewell he took his image seriously. If one day he played professional baseball or even coached in high school, he wanted everyone around him to feel good that he was a friend. To say the least, he was a likable guy that everyone wanted to be around.

While he is recovering at the hospital, his friends come by, most knowing they will not be able to see him because he is in the Intensive Care Unit. They came to be together and lend whatever support they could to his family. They came together to talk. They came to find out firsthand how this man, one who had achieved so much success on the gridiron, the court and the diamond, they came to find out how he was going to handle this situation. Some are worried that since he will never throw a baseball again that it will kill him. Cory thought about that too. He had thrown, kicked, or shot a ball every day of his life that he could remember. Now, he was faced with not even being able to grip a baseball. It wasn't something he dwelled on. Others worried that the injuries are so massive that the change in his life will cripple his ability to be Cory, their fun loving friend. And others came because they genuinely cared about this man and want him to know that they will be there for him in the future.

Football training camp will be starting in a week. Several of Cory's college friends are sitting around his bed watching TV with him. He is tilted up on the rotating bed, only able to see the TV through a mirror. It is awkward for them to talk with him through the halo, the straps, the monitors. Cory finds a way to make them comfortable. One of his favorites is, "I have a headache. Oh no wonder. They tightened the screws in my skull this morning." Others are "I can honestly say that I am screwed up in the head." His favorite to ease the situation is, "I don't have to go to a psychiatrist to get screwed up in the head."

Phyllis enters the room. All of his buddies like Phyllis because of her good looks and quick wit. Cory sees her and says "I bet none of you guys get a bath every day from someone who looks like Phyllis?"

They laugh but she is quick to reply "Watch it buddy, your injury won't kill you now, but if I don't take extra time with certain parts, the crotch rot will surely kill you."

It sends the whole room into a roar. They can't help but chide Cory about his "private(s) nurse."

Denney Fales is a friend from Smithville. He will prove to be one of Cory's longest lasting friends. On this day, Denney is reading the cards that are hanging on the wall. He watered the plants and trashed the old balloons that had one time stood at the end of their strings but where now hanging down to the floor. Denney continues kidding him and keeping his spirits up as he cleans the room. "I didn't think I'd ever be cleaning up after you Wohlford. You're the relief pitcher." They both momentarily think about Cory's not so distant past memories on the mound. Denney grows quiet. Cory cracks him up with "Get the vacuum. You're not finished."

As the bed tilts, it keeps the pressure off of the same parts of Cory's body. If he lays too long in one spot, the circulation stops and the pressure point could become a sore. Cory wouldn't feel the sores, but if infected, he could get very sick and in a weakened state it could kill him. So the bed keeps tilting.

Denney grabs a deck of cards and notes that the baseball game they want to watch doesn't start for an hour. Cory's friends gather around a small table that Denney brought in from the waiting room. He deals the cards then helps Cory play his cards in a spirited game of spades. Phyllis likes it. Even though he can't reach out and play the card, his friend Denney is there to help.

Cory is known for his card playing. The many miles he has ridden across the country in the back of a team bus led him to be a great card player. He always thought several plays ahead and had a strategy for every one of his cards. He knew what cards will most likely be played and when. This was always to his advantage and something he loved to do when playing sports. He carries his *on the field thinking* to the card table and kicks everyone's butt to their screams of "no mercy."

Friends have been important throughout Cory's life. His best friends are his brothers Chris and Steve. It helped them play together on the athletic field. Cory knew he could count on his brothers. This innate ability made them the ultimate example of team work. Their many years of throwing the ball in the yard and shooting baskets didn't hurt. They had played ball every day. When they got tired of pitching and hitting, they started shooting at that old rim that was bolted to light pole in the driveway. Cory had a great arm for football and baseball. Chris had a great shot for basketball and could hit a baseball a mile. Steve rounded out the team with strength and desire. He wasn't as tall as the twins, but he worked just as hard and when all three are on the field, their opponents took notice.

CHAPTER 27

Revelation – Fall 1985

Cory has gotten stronger from all of the hard exercise the therapists have been giving him. When he slows down or cops an attitude, Phyllis or Ginger are right there to cheer him on. They don't take no for an answer and are quick witted to match Cory.

He had always been great with the girls because of his endearing qualities and good looks. It didn't work with Phyllis. She loved him for what he is and the hard work he had put in to get him from the bed into a wheelchair. She watched in despair as his finely tuned body started to dwindle because it lacked the training he had put himself through all during his career. She also smiled, knowing that he is alive because of this physical strength and the way he was brought up.

Cory didn't want to work out the next day. The therapists wanted him to lift more weight and work out longer. Normally this time of year he is lifting a bar with hundreds of pounds of lead slapped on each end. He spent hours doing it in the weight room. Now, the little ten pound weights suspended on ropes through pulleys are starting to get the best of him. He tries hard and tries some more. He definitely didn't want his little brother Steve to see him struggling with these small weights. Steve had been the strongest of the boys getting the bulk in his frame and his barrel chest from Big Jon.

His workout over, the therapists wheeled him back to his room. Phyllis had the day off and her replacement hadn't brought lunch. They placed him near the window, the halo an ever reminder that his injury is nothing to be taken lightly. As the day wears on he snaps at Becky because she is late, immediately saying he is sorry.

Later Jon and Cory are the only two in the room. Jon has been reading to Cory out of the Bible. Cory is crying and suddenly a look of rage comes over his face. He is mad at God for his condition. Why him? He should be sprinting up hills and keeping his body in top shape. Instead he can barely lift the small weights on the ropes. He lets the phone ring, even though he knows it is Chris, just wanting to say hi.

Cory is sitting by the window late that night. The room is dimly lit. He has been there all afternoon and didn't eat much for dinner. After Becky and Jon left in the early evening, Cory is alone. He is talking to someone, but no one is around. He pulls his hands up and holds them to the heavens, his fingers unable to open. When he listened to the letter from Cheryl Green he thought it was a nice gesture, just like everyone else. Tonight he has no one else to talk with so he takes her advice and is talking to God. His eyes are closed and his face is animated.

Cory turns his wheelchair with a look of determination and suddenly as if breaking a football huddle, rolls toward a nurse that had just walked in. She steps behind him and pushes him to his now familiar bed. That night he gets the best night sleep since his accident. He is ready to heal having found the mystery of recovery despite the massive injury. He strengthens his will to live, to overcome his suffering and start healing. The Lord has given him this opportunity to live a full life and fulfill his dreams. He is ready.

It's morning when Cory opens his eyes. He knows the therapists have a full day planned and Phyllis will keep her regular routine of pushing him to the limits. Today is different. He is looking forward to a meeting with Dr. Whitaker this morning. He has been a strong advocate for Cory since he was brought in from the helicopter. His talk with God the night before lifted his spirits. He knows the battle ahead will be ongoing, but that he is on Gods side and that makes his life worth living. It is time for him to get on with it.

Jon and Becky enter his room followed by Dr. Whitaker. Becky sits on the edge of his bed. Jon and Dr. Whitaker sit in chairs across from Cory. Chris and Steve come in and sit down on the couch.

The Doctor has called the meeting so he could give them an update on Cory's condition and prepare them for the future.

"Since Cory has been here, he has taught us a lot about how important one's attitude is. He can move on now."

Dr. Whitaker had been prepping Cory for his next journey. Cory knows that time is close. Today they will find out if Craig had space for the three months it will take Cory to learn to live in a wheelchair.

Cory is concerned. How are his parents going to afford to go to Colorado for three months?

"Craig Hospital has accepted you. It's just outside of Denver and they have a great staff" he continues.

Jon added "Your Nurse Susan has told us good stuff about Craig. We are looking forward to getting Cory out there."

Dr. Whitaker nods, and then looks hard at Cory, "I have watched you work hard. Continue that out in Colorado. Air Care is set up to fly you out, so enjoy the ride."

Becky, Jon and Dr. Whitaker stand and Becky gives the Doctor a strong and grateful hug and whispers a heartfelt "Thank you." "It has been my pleasure to get to know you. I admire your family and how you have pulled it together. Now it is time to look forward to a bright and exciting future."

Dr. Whitaker goes toward the door. He stops when he hears Cory's voice. "Thank you Doctor.... for everything."

When the door is closed Cory asks Big Jon "How are we going to afford this? Insurance won't cover everything."

Jon smiles, he is thinking the same. The last couple of months really tapped them and with having three sons in college, expenses are already high. Now, the cost of the hospital and their living expenses while they are in Colorado learning how to take care of Cory's needs, are heavy on all of them. Jon and Becky are going to take on a new role beyond parents. They will share the duties of caretaker. Just like Cory going to Craig to learn how to live within his abilities, they too will learn how to take care of him. Cory is a big man and it will take both of them to meet his care requirements.

Jon looked at his son with his bushy eyebrows raised.

"You don't worry about that. The Lord will take care of us Cory. We will be there for you."

They are partners taking care of Cory all the rest of Big Jon's life.

CHAPTER 28

Replacement: William Jewell Football 1985

Chris and Jon are sitting watching the Royals on TV. Having time to relax with Chris is a treat for Jon. The last month had taken him away from the other boys and he is anxious to get caught up. Jon kept asking about the details of the baseball games he had been playing.

Jon notices that Chris is preoccupied and the more he asks him about the last few weeks of baseball, the more Chris looked uncomfortable. Finally Jon asked him what was wrong.

"I'm glad that Cory is going to Colorado. They can teach him some good things there."

"They sure can. It will be hard on your Mother, not being able to see him."

Chris leans forward, putting his elbows on his knees and looks down. "I have been thinking and I am going to try out to take Cory's place on the football team." Chris looks up for approval from his father.

Jon slowly replies. "Why?"

"I have a year of eligibility left. Basketball and Baseball are over for me but I still have one year to play football."

Jon looks at him, trying to comprehend the issue. His reply is sharp and calculated. "You haven't played football in four years. What makes you think you can make it?"

Chris stands, towering over his father. His voice is strong and full of conviction. "Because I will be playing for Cory. People will continue to remember Cory and all those good thoughts and prayers will help heal him."

Jon stands and gives his strong son a hug. A joyful chuckle in his voice, "I think that is a good thing Chris. I'm sure that Cory will think so too." He grabs him by the shoulders and looks eye to eye with him. "You are a good son."

Ten days later, after training on his own every day, Chris walks into the Cardinal Football locker room for the first time as a player. When he takes the field for the first practice, all of the players and coaches applaud and wish him luck. When he breaks into the starting lineup, they all realize the value of his commitment. With his success, they understand that he is not playing for himself. He is playing for Cory.

CHAPTER 29

To Cory with Love

The Wohlford family attends the First Christian Church of Smithville. Even though they went to Plattsburg schools, the home place is nearest to Smithville where Becky's family lives and attends the church. When the boys are in high school they regularly attended the church. Jon and Becky sat on the second row from the back and the boys would sit with the Davidson twins and their little brother at the back of the church, on couches in the parlor. Unless a visitor found the couches, the Wohlford and Davidson boys are regulars there. Before the service they compare notes on the latest victories at both Plattsburg and Smithville.

The Church is at full capacity and very quiet. On this Sunday, one of the boys is missing. Families are all sitting close and Denney Fales, one of Cory's closest friends, is sitting with the Wohlfords. Becky's family members are longtime members of the church family and they are all there.

The Pastor's sermon is short today. He has an important issue to deal with and will need everyone in the congregation to help.

"In closing today, everyone here knows Jon and Becky, Chris and Steve Wohlford."

He looks out at Jon, Becky, Chris, and Steve who are sitting on the aisle near the middle of the church

"...and we all know that their son and brother Cory broke his neck in a car accident this summer and is paralyzed. Many of you have given support, food, and donations. The Wohlford family has asked me to thank you for your encouragement and support. Cory continues to get better. He is strong in his spirit and has faith that the Lord has special meaning for his life. When I spoke with him this week he said to tell you this 'he has received'...the congregation is stirring, wet eyes everywhere. '...so much love from family and friends with such big hearts. He now realizes it's time to begin his life again from the start. Time has gone by and his next journey is about to begin. This new challenge is here, deep down he thinks he is gonna win. His inner strength will not let him fail at this new task. Tell my church family and all that can hear thank you from the bottom of my heart.' There is a pause as many in the congregation are wiping tears from their eyes.

"We have been updating you on Cory's condition each week. The 'To Cory with Love Fund' has been set up to help Cory with medical expenses. You can make donations by dropping off a donation to the church office or simply drop it in the offering plate each Sunday. This is a great way to show Cory our love for him."

Jon and Becky are looking around the room, meeting the eyes of their Church family with gracious hearts. Everyone is nodding in support and admiration.

"Cory was being transferred to Craig Hospital in Inglewood, Colorado. There, he has continued with his rehabilitation as they teach him how to live in a wheelchair. All of our prayers are with Cory as he begins this new journey. The communities of Plattsburg and Smithville have come together to help Cory with an outpouring of love that is incredible. His friend Denney Fales led the charge in helping organize a softball tournament that raised over three thousand dollars and a golf tournament raised another twenty five hundred. The Plattsburg Student Council held a special dance and the Teachers Association is selling programs at football games. They played a basketball tournament in Plattsburg. There have been Tupperware parties. Booster clubs, Rotary Clubs. There have been bazaars, bake sales and flower sales. Other churches in our community have made donations. Everyone who knows Cory and his family know what a special young man he is. Let us pray." All heads in the room bow in prayer. The Wohlford family is holding hands.

"Dear Lord, We see the strength of our community in the incredible ways they have supported Cory Wohlford and his family in this, their time of need. You are the maker of all good things, so we ask you to watch over this family, giving them strength as they journey to Colorado tomorrow. Protect and guide them. We ask you to bless them and comfort them, inspire and hold them. Let our love go with them and give them comfort. Amen."

The next morning Jon and Becky are excited to get on their way. Arrangements have been made with a family in Colorado to provide them with a bedroom in their home. The Lord is providing for them, just like Jon and Cory read in the Bible.

They are excited about seeing Cory again. It has been a long couple of months and they are eager to see their son and how he has progressed.

Trees are turning brilliant reds and oranges as the fall days grow short. It is a rainy cool morning as they leave the farm, packed for the month ahead where they will learn how to help Cory maximize his abilities. Driving through the village of Trimble they pull up to a STOP sign on 169 Highway. They both look to their right where a woman is approaching their car waving frantically. They recognize Wilma French from Church as Becky rolls down her window.

"Jon, Becky. We know you are going to have expenses in Colorado. Here is some money from the 'To Cory with Love' fund from the Church. God bless you."

Jon and Becky are emotionally overcome. Jon slowly replies. "We can't tell you how much we appreciate this."

"You don't need to. Just send our love to Cory."

"Thank you Wilma. Tell everyone we are so grateful for this."

In a low and scratchy voice she replies, "Have a safe trip and tell Cory we miss him. Good bye." Wilma steps back, her handkerchief dabbing her eyes and a look of admiration on her face.

Jon and Becky drive away waving and smiling. Becky opens the package and looks inside. She turns to Jon.

"Jon, this envelope is full of money. We are so blessed. Thank you Lord for our wonderful friends and church family."

"It certainly helps. Thank God" says Jon as he points the car toward Denver.

CHAPTER 30

Training Camp

Cory is being wheeled into the Main Entrance at Craig Hospital after enjoying an hour in the brilliant sunlight. He is met by several good looking nurses. They are joking and trying to make him feel comfortable. Dressed in jeans and polo shirts, Deborah, a strong and beautiful nurse grabs his wheelchair and pushes him down the hall to his room. He has been there long enough that many of them are his friends. They also know of his athletic history and trade barbs with him about different teams in college and pros and especially about the Royals winning the World Series. Cory likes them all. They kid that he will watch paint dry if it has a final score.

Later in the afternoon something is different. The TV is not on. Cory has a phone cradled up to his ear and listening intently. Deborah enters the room loudly.

"You ready to go up to see Lisa in therapy Mister?"

Cory keeps his concentration on the phone and without looking he replies. "Not now. Chris is playing football against Baker. They are our rival. The guys at his fraternity called and the game is on the radio there."

Cory looks up sheepishly to see if he is in trouble for the response.

"Let's see if I can get you in later." He thanks her and turns his attention back to the phone. They didn't have the Internet or massive cable system like today, so this is the best way for Cory to stay in touch and hear the game.

It is late in the game and the William Jewell Cardinals are ahead by two points 30-28. Baker has the ball on the William Jewell 40 yard line and is driving. They are trying to get close enough for a field goal and win the game. Chris has been playing a great game. The announcers have talked about his play all afternoon.

The Baker Quarterback runs an option to the right, pitching at the final moment. Chris, wearing number five, comes up from his safety position and makes a ferocious hit on the ball carrier. The announcer says "That was some hit for a two yard loss by the William Jewell Safety Cory Wohlford. Correction that is Chris Wohlford, Cory's twin brother."

The other announcer chips in "That's right and he has come on to lead the Cardinals this year while his twin brother Cory is out with a serious neck injury."

On the next play Chris has dropped back into pass coverage. The speedy Baker flanker is racing down the middle of the field as the Quarterback throws a high long pass over the middle. It is a foot race between Chris and the Flanker. Chris out jumps the receiver and intercepts the ball, then runs it back to mid-field.

"That will seal up this victory for the Cardinals" they announce.

Chris comes off the field holding the ball high. He is mobbed as he gets close to the sideline. His teammates all crowd around him as he repeats over and over "This one is for Cory."

Cory has the phone cradled to his ear, as his attractive physical therapist Lisa comes in the door.

"What's this I hear about you breaking our date" she says.

Cory pays no attention, intent on the phone. "You have to get me the game film. They said Chris had eight tackles and an interception. What? I can't hear. OK. Just a few more minutes. I'd like to hear the post game."

Back at William Jewell the game has ended and players are walking off the field. Chris is still holding the game ball. A reporter approaches him for a live, on-air interview.

"You had eight tackles, three for losses, broke up two passes, and intercepted a pass at the end of the game to secure a Cardinal victory. Tell us about it."

Chris replies "It was a good game. The whole team played well."

"You are wearing number five this year. Tell us the significance of that number."

"It is in honor my brother."

Cory is listening on the telephone. His heart is full with love for his brother.

"Your fraternity brothers rigged up a special phone line so Cory could hear the game. Is there anything you want to say to him?"

The Reporter is standing beside Chris while players and fans gather around.

"The team dedicated this season to Cory. Everyone here is praying for you Cory. I have the game ball for you and when you get off that airplane next month, expect to get a hand off."

Cory puts the phone down, feeling joy and pride. Lisa comforts him with a close hug.

"Are you Ok?" she asks.

"Yea, I am OK. They won and Chris had a great year."

"Why are you upset?"

He looks at her and says "I'm not upset. I am happy. They dedicated the season to me, and Chris had the best game of his career. He even intercepted a pass at the end of the game and saved the ball for me."

"That is wonderful Cory. Congratulations. I can come back later." Cory replies "No way. Let's get going. We have got a lot of work to do."

Later in the workout room Cory is being put through a tough rehabilitation exercise by Lisa. As he continues to work different exercises he feels himself getting stronger. He is focused on maximizing the abilities he has and not worrying about what he can't do. The months have passed fast as evidenced by the patches of snow on the ground and frost on the windows.

Cory is nearing the end of his stay. Lisa and Cory are sitting at a table eating lunch. Cory has a contraption on his hand that helps him hold his spoon.

"So you are headed home tomorrow. Are you excited?" she asks. "You bet" he replies as he stops and admires her beauty for a moment. She looks at him and he smiles. "I am going to miss you Cory" "I'll miss you too. You have been kicking my butt for three months. Honestly, you have really made my stay here special. Teaching me how to live with all these props has helped both my mind and body. You have a special gift" replies Cory.

"No Cory, I am really going to miss you. You are a great friend... Let's get you back to your room. Its late and you need your rest."

In his room Lisa is finishing putting Cory to bed. She then sits on the edge of the bed. "I have never had a patient that has given it their all like you have." "I didn't know there was any other way. And besides, I had a great coach!" he laughs. Lisa continues "I wish you love and happiness. Some girl out there deserves a man like you."

She hugs Cory softly. As she goes out the door she looks back and says, "Thank you Cory. I'll miss you."

CHAPTER 31

Homecoming – February 1986

It is an unusually warm day for February in Kansas City. The sun has broken through and three weeks of cloudy skies is now replaced by the powder blue sky of a warm winter day. Today, Cory is coming home from the Craig Hospital. It has been over six months since the accident. Now he eagerly anticipates getting home to the farm.

Leaving the hospital had been hard because of the wonderful people that had put their hearts and souls into his rehabilitation. They in turn admired Cory for the courage and dedication he put forth every day. There are ups and downs with the routine and learning. He learned how to deal with his limits. When it came time to leave, those bonds of trust and admiration go with him.

The hospital corridor is filled with the therapists, nurses, technicians, and Doctors that had worked with Cory. Big Jon is there to push him down the hall. Hugs and kisses are mixed with all the well wishes. They had all seen him come in the door, scared and unknowing of his future. Now they are proud of the young man from Missouri who had worked so hard to get his life back. His gratitude is evidenced by the parting smiles and words of thanks he gave them. As they came to the door and their final goodbyes, Cory sees the one person he wanted to thank the most. Lisa is standing on the front lawn. It was her day off, but she needed to see him one more time. As he approached her in his chair, she stood looking at him. He rolled right up next to her. A knot is in his throat and he isn't able to say anything. She pulls him close and puts her head on his shoulder one last time. No words could ever express the feelings of admiration. She just looked softly at him, touched his soul, and slowly walked away.

On the way to the airport the butterflies in Cory's stomach matched any he had before the big games of his career. He had been looking forward to the bitter sweet departure and anticipating what might be waiting for him at home. His heart raced as the van pulled up to Stapleton Airport. They quickly unloaded him and for the first time he is thrust into a massive crowd of people. The airport is filled with people heading to the mountains for ski vacations, business people in their wool winter suits and families being reunited. He is looking around to see if people are staring at him. Other than a few little kids that look with wonder, he is being treated like anyone else. Sure they had to give him more room to move around, but he found that everyone is respectful and try to help as he slowly negotiated the crowd.

Getting to the gate, his wait is short. The flight attendants and gate personnel had been specifically trained to get people in wheel chairs on board incredibly fast and easy. He is the first on and the last off the plane.

The butterflies built as the plane left the runway on that beautiful blue Colorado morning. The ride above the snowy plains of Kansas is smooth as he looked out the window at the rolling fields of farmland and the flint hills of the central plains. Having the halo off now, the torn muscles mended and strengthened, he is able to move his head. The flight is a little more than an hour. Cory noted later that this hour had been one of the shortest in his life. He didn't know what to anticipate when he arrived home. He had learned how to live in a wheel chair, feed himself and the things he will need others to insure he is able to survive. Many things are going through his head. What worried him most is how his friends and family will look at him now. He is still the same person, just in a different package. He is afraid that he could never have a relationship with a woman. How will he meet them and how can someone dedicate the time and effort to love him so unconditionally. Will they be able to take care of his needs? How is he going to make a living? Were all his friends going to "be there" as they claimed in their cards and letters? How is he going to get around in the old two story farmhouse? They didn't have a bathroom that his chair fit into. All these questions swirled in his head until the plane touched down at Kansas City International Airport and taxied to the terminal.

He could see the glass walls of the terminal from the plane as he waited for the other passengers. What he couldn't anticipate is what lay beyond.

They transferred him from the large First Class seat to his chair. There stood Big Jon, smiling from ear to ear. He is getting his son home and his feelings of joy could not be contained. Jon pushed him up the ramp and around the corner of the jet way into the terminal. He stopped at the top of the jet way and grabbed Cory's shoulder from behind. With two words, "Welcome Home," and in a few more steps Cory saw a crowd of people. Pictures are snapped. Confetti flies. Signs are hoisted. Familiar faces of family, friends, teammates, and coaches crowded the terminal. Cheers went up as they saw Big Jon push him through the door and through the crowd. Other passengers stopped and wondered what famous person was on the plane who garnered this much attention. News cameras are set up so as not to interfere. They recorded the moment of true jubilation as a favorite son returned home.

Chris and Steve told their friends he was coming home. Chris had sent him the Red Cardinal Jersey with the number five on it for the trip. Everyone knew the date and time he was to arrive. No one anticipated this large of a crowd. People lined both sides of the terminal clearing a way for Big Jon to push Cory slowly through. Everyone wanted to touch Cory and give him cards and well wishes. They are saying how proud they are of him.

Chris steps forward, holding a football above his head. It is the game ball from the William Jewell football game against Baker University, he had heard on the telephone.

"One more thing. Cory, the team wants you to have this. You deserve it more than anyone."

Chris hands Cory the game ball and the crowd breaks into applause.

He eagerly anticipated getting home but wanted to say hi to everyone. As they filed by, Jon slowly inched him toward the door and the waiting van. Once outside, Cory feels the warmth of the sun. It is nothing compared to the warmth he feels in his heart and the game ball he holds in his lap.

"One day soon you'll have a van like this that you can drive yourself," forecasts Jon as they load him for the ride home.

Sitting in his strapped down chair in the back of the van, Cory is able to recognize the fields and highways around the airport. Soon they are smoothly running down the highway on their thirty minute ride home. Cory keeps pointing out the landmarks and recalling the memories of eating at the restaurants and filling his car with gas at the One Stop.

Then he says "Dad, I am nervous about going home."

Jon knew he would be. "No need. We have made a lot of changes. You'll see."

As they pull into the driveway, calm settles over Cory as he is grateful to be home. Streamers and crepe paper line the doorway. Next to the driveway stands a wooden sawhorse with a sign on it. "Welcome Home Cory" had been stenciled onto a large poster and attached to the sawhorse. Behind it is another sign attached to the house. "We are glad you are home."

Cory gets unloaded from the van. A ramp has been built to the side porch door and a new larger door has been installed.

"We would have painted it for you but it's been too darn cold" says Steve as he approvingly swings the door open for Cory. "You'll just have one of your girlfriends do it one of these days," he jokes.

Once inside Cory notices that many changes have been made. Most important is the addition of a large bathroom off the kitchen. It is specifically designed to accommodate him. His bedroom is now the parlor room. The first floor room allowed him access to the kitchen and bath through the dining room and direct access to the large living room. Jon and Becky had thought of everything that he will need and then they worked day and night to get it done before he came home. Even the wallpaper is new.

Cory is happy to be home.

CHAPTER 32

A Million Words

Winter turned into spring. Cory enjoyed sitting on the east porch watching the wildlife both near and far away. The porch gave him an unobstructed view of the hills rolling down to Smithville Lake. He could see the deer feeding on the left over corn laid low in the fields. He watched the flights of the large predatory birds as they flew in circles above their prey of rabbits and squirrels. Rabbits bounded through the yard eating fresh clover. Squirrels scampered up and down the big oak trees in the yard and the nearby walnut trees they depended on for their winter food.

The farm is alive with activity as the fields are plowed and prepared for planting. The garden is tilled and Cory rolls out to watch as Becky and Jon plant the tomatoes, rows of corn and beans, cucumbers, lettuce, beets and potatoes. He especially likes the zucchini and melons. They will grow, reaching out with their vines with blossoms turning into little nubs, then growing and filling the garden with a hundred or more of their fruit.

During the day he reads a lot and watches TV. In the evening friends drop in and they talk and play games. After a year of adjusting to his new life he decided it was time to go back and finish his degree. It will also give him the chance to connect with old friends and meet some girls. William Jewell had already made their campus comply with the Americans with Disabilities Act and every building is accessible.

College is not quite the same this time around. The classes seemed easier. He got higher grades in harder classes. He didn't have the commitment to team practices for football and baseball or the continued physical training schedule required to compete at the highest level. Nor did he have the travel schedule for baseball that took him from his classes every spring. Without these distractions and a few late night frat parties, now he had the time to really digest the material and understand it versus the old way of learning the highlights and hoping what he studied is on the test. He enjoys being around old friends and making new ones.

During his last semester, part of his day is student teaching at a high school. He applied at several schools so when he got the call from Diana Tingler, the Girls Basketball Coach and Physical Education Teacher at Smithville, he was delighted. Diana had often seen Cory play football, basketball, and baseball as a member of the Smithville coaching staff. She knows in her heart he will be a good candidate for student teaching and was glad he accepted. The many friends he had in Smithville were very supportive and just like everything Cory did, he poured himself into the position.

After a year of school and student teaching, he is ready to graduate. William Jewell is a beautiful campus in a grove of old growth trees sitting high above the Liberty Square, County Seat of Clay County, Missouri. Its red brick buildings are connected across a campus of manicured lawns. The buildings are designed for intimate classroom settings and spacious comfortable halls.

On this Sunday, the graduation hall is crowded with a large stage rising across the end. The President of William Jewell is handing out diplomas. Steve has finished his degree and Cory is now graduating in the same class. They are slowly approaching the top of the ramp in their caps and gowns. The President called Steve's name and handed him his diploma as he walked across the stage.

Then the President stopped. It was unusual because all of the speeches had been made and this was the finality of the ceremony. Cory realizes that with the last name Wohlford, alphabetically there is no one behind him, and he is in the middle of the stage by himself.

"I want to take a moment to recognize our next graduate. Cory Wohlford suffered a severe and debilitating injury. He was a member of our Football and Baseball teams where he excelled at both sports. Most expected him to go on further in baseball or coach. I would like to personally acknowledge the strength, devotion, and persistence of Cory Wohlford to come back and finish his degree."

The audience gives Cory a long, standing ovation. As it starts to subside he rolls toward the center of the stage expecting to get his diploma when the President speaks directly to him. "A lesser man would have folded. A lesser man would have never come back. This diploma tells everyone that you are truly a winner. You look adversity in the eye every day and every day you win."

Becky and Jon are proudly sitting near the front with Chris. "The baseball team missed you. The football team missed you. Your friends missed you. You have come back with a vengeance. You came back to the classroom, did your student teaching, and finished what you started." The applause started again. "I was speaking with Coach Wallace earlier today and he told me that you have talked about a comeback. Getting back on the field.... to coach. I am going to steal Coach Wallace's thunder. Let me be the first to congratulate you. Next season you will join the team as a defensive coach."

More applause.

"Winning is contagious and I hope that everyone here sees your example and learns to win at their endeavors."

The applause starts up again.

"Cory Wohlford, it is with great honor and humbleness that I present you with this degree."

Cory accepts the degree, rolls off of the stage to a standing ovation where he meets Steve dressed in a gown and holding his diploma. He gets a hug from Steve as the ovation continues.

The class of graduates stands still with many of them motioning for Cory to lead them out of the hall. He heads his chair down the aisle as everyone continues their applause and turns their heads with looks of admiration as he rolls by.

CHAPTER 33

Winning as a Warrior - 1988

Bill Maas had been the high school Football Coach at Smithville for six years. Every year he prepared a team to make a run at the conference and district championships. He was successful winning them both. He was known as a compassionate and good coach in the community as well as a good person. He knew how to handle boys and his own three were growing up to be good men. His youngest will play on a National Championship football team in college.

Coach Maas is very temperamental in the selection of his coaches. He wants the best experience for his boys and knows that a bad coach could bring down the whole team. He knows Big Jon quite well. Big Jon had been selling sporting goods, uniforms, and supplies to the school for years and he had even known him when he had been the coach at Savannah High School. During his first year as a coach at Smithville, he felt the strength of the Wohlford twins as they beat a very good Smithville team on their way to a State Championship. He was also the Athletic Director for the school so he was at nearly every varsity sporting event. He had been at the buzzer beater game in Plattsburg when Cory and Chris beat a great Smithville basketball team. He knew the Wohlford family and even though they did not go to Smithville schools, they are very visible in the community with their family members who lived in Smithville.

Today he is with Rod Hart, the longtime Head Basketball Coach and teacher at Smithville High School. They are sitting at the conference table in the Board of Education room at the school. Bill is leaning back in his chair with his hands folded.

"So you think Cory can handle coaching football with the heat and cold we go through?"

Rod replied, "I have known him for years. I don't know if he is able to tolerate the heat being over a hundred degrees when you start camp and falling off to below zero by the time you finish in the fall. I will tell you one thing Cory will give it his best. He is great inspiration for the kids. Bill, you know this is the right thing to do. He coached at Jewell last year. I think he will be just fine"

"He is substituting for Bill Reynolds today and I have asked him to stop by" says Coach Maas with a slight grin on his face.

There is a knock on the door as it swings open. Diane Tingler steps into the room

"You wanted to see me?" and sits down.

"Hi Diane. I want your opinion about a Coach that has asked to join our football staff. What do you think about Cory coaching football?"

She lights up, a smile crosses her face and she replies "That is a great idea Bill. He was one of the best student teachers I have ever had. He relates so well to the kids. Just to see him interact with the kids makes you realize he was born to coach. I wholly endorse Cory as a coach but I am biased because I really like Cory as a person."

Coach Hart leans in "He has come in several times to talk to my driver's education classes about driving too fast and driving without a seat belt. It gives them a chance to see what can happen if they are stupid with a car."

"I know how you feel Diane. I really like Cory and his family. The problem is we don't have the money in the budget for another coach. Any suggestions?"

"You could ask him to volunteer. I am sure there is some way that we can get help to pay his expenses then maybe next year he can get paid."

"You keep winning Bill and putting people in the stands, next year you will have enough in the budget. Either way, I am sure he would be honored just to be asked." Coach Tingler agrees. "Then you both agree he is capable and wouldn't be insulted if we can't pay him this year?"

They all agree when there is another knock on the door and Cory pushes it open and enters. "You wanted to see me. Is it about the coaching? I can understand if you decide no. I'll still help you break down film and other stuff. Anything will be fine."

"Yeah Cory. Pull on up here. We were just talking about you" says Coach Maas putting on his coaching hat.

"I am not being called into the Principals office because I am in trouble am I?" They all laugh.

"No Cory. Not this time anyway. I am wondering if you are interested in helping me coach the football team. But before you answer you need to know that this is not a paid position this year. I need help from a guy who has a football mind like yours. You can bring the latest football strategies from college to our program."

"It sounds great, but I need to make sure that I, we, Mom and Dad can make the commitment."

Coach replies "Take your time. We don't need to know today."

"Thank you for thinking of me."

Cory turns with a look of excitement on his face as he goes out the door. They all smile because they know that a valuable new coach could be joining their staff.

Getting to and from places is hard for Cory. His friends have come through in a big way. When he needed to go to school, Denney Fales is there. Greg Summers took him to Football practice and games, and also to therapy in Kansas City by removing the tops out of his Trans-Am. They were always there to get him around before he got his van. Now Cory can get around on his own.

CHAPTER 33

Brother versus Brother - 1991

Cory had been coaching at Smithville for three years. The team was successful every year. He is able to influence the type of running and passing game they are using and well known for. He had coached a couple of years on offense then switched to defense depending on the role he was needed in.

Cory has always dreamed of being a head coach but knows that type of commitment would be hard for a school board to make. In Missouri most coaches teach full time to be a Head Coach. It would be almost impossible for Cory to be in his wheel chair for an eight hour school day, then coach for a couple of hours and do game prep. It would be physically impossible and Cory knew it. Right now the Smithville coaching position fits him just fine.

Chris has gone on to a successful career coaching also. He was now on the coaching staff for Lawson High School. They are a division rival of Smithville and a tough competitor year in and year out. This year is no different because both teams field experienced teams.

Tonight it is brother against brother in a football game that is reminiscent of the Freeman brothers' games back in the 1980's. It is the first time that Cory and Chris are coaching for opposing teams. They are at the Smithville High School stadium. Chris is dressed in Cardinal Red and Cory is dressed in Warrior Green. They are at midfield, with Cory in his wheelchair. Chris and Cory are laughing and joking. Chris says "I finally get a shot at you brother."

"You know Chris that the last time we were on the football field together we were holding a State Championship trophy?"

Chris replied "Those were the glory days" as he shifts the conversation to the present. "Your boys are playing well. You look good on film."

"We got by that loss against Platte County and have been getting better every week. You better watch out, I have a couple of trick plays we have been working on" Cory warned.

Chris says "We're using Coach Freeman's three yards and a cloud of dust offense. He refereed our game against Lathrop last week."

"He said you threw that screen play for the touchdown to beat them" responds Cory. Chris puts his hands on his hips and spins toward his team in a mock display of displeasure.

"I can't believe it; you have Jim Freeman scouting for you now?"

Cory straightens himself in his chair, then smiles. "The only thing Jim Freeman tells me about coaching is, "Teamwork wins...." and they finish the sentence together "Championships"

Chris looks to the Smithville sideline. "Hey, they got your pedestal set up back there. Looks like a good spot to watch us beat you."

Chris points to large box made of angle iron with a platform about three foot off the ground. It had been made by Mr. Schuler and the Future Farmers of America blue jackets at the High School.

"You wait. We're ready for the Cardinals."

Chris knows he has his team ready and replies "Anything is possible. We have a good shot at beating you. What is it now, five straight district championships?"

"We plan on making it six." Cory replies.

"We'll see you after the game."

Cory turns and wheels toward the offensive team that has started to run plays, while Chris walks over to his team with another coach walking beside him.

One of the Cardinal's coaches admires Cory "He's a good guy."

"The best. I don't think I could have gone through what he has been through and still be out here." Chris stops, slowly turns and watches Cory at the other end of the field for a moment, a look of admiration

172

on his face. Instinctively Cory turns, sees his brother and smiles. The game is on.

The teams finish their warm up and go to the sidelines to start the game. Cory is in the middle of the Smithville huddle.

"The team that plays as a team for the whole game will be the team that wins. My brother Chris coaches them and we won a State Championship because we played as a team. Now go play as a team."

The team breaks the huddle and Cory rolls over to the sideling beside the platform followed by the entire coaching staff. He positions himself behind the platform with a group of players and coaches around him. The coaches all squat down and lift his chair up onto the platform. The fans in the bleachers all applaud.

The game is being broadcast on a Kansas City radio station as the game of the week. Both teams come into the game with outstanding records. Smithville stands at 4-1 and the reigning District Sixteen champion, while Lawson is undefeated and ranked fifth in the State of Missouri. These two teams go at it every year with the winner usually ending up in the state playoffs.

The announcer starts his interpretation of the game with a little background on the teams. "Coach Matt Henshaw leads the Warriors. On his staff is one of my favorites, Cory Wohlford. Many of you may recognize Cory from his perch on the sideline. He was paralyzed in a car accident a number of years ago while playing football and baseball at William Jewell College. Adding to the story is Chris Wohlford, Cory's twin brother who is on the Lawson coaching staff. The Wohlford brothers played on the 1979 Plattsburg State Championship team. I called that game in St. Louis and the whole town was there as the Plattsburg Tigers won 12-7 over a highly touted Marceline team."

The other announcer chirped in "As I recall, these brothers were key to the Tigers win and now they face each other."

Both teams are on the field. Smithville won the toss and will receive. Lawson kicks the ball off and Smithville makes a good return. Their offense is running on all cylinders as they score on their first possession. Cory is smiling and laughing as he talks to the coaches on his headset. The kick is no good and the score is Smithville 6 – Lawson 0 with four minutes to go in the First quarter.

Throughout the game Cory is talking to the coaches through the headset and to players as he calls them over to the pedestal.

Chris is on the Lawson sideline talking with his defensive backs and line backers while drawing on a small white board. On the Smithville sideline Cory is high above the players on the pedestal looking over his clip board at plays and formations to use, between watching the defensive backs on the field and calling out defensive signals in his headset.

Lawson scores on a screen pass at the start of the second quarter, the kick is no go and the scoreboard shows Smithville 6 - Lawson 6.

Cory is having an animated conversation with one of his defensive backs as the half time score stands tied.

The Smithville coaches come over to the stand and lower Cory to the ground. The Coaches all walk together around Cory discussing the strategy for the second half before getting to the locker room.

Smithville scores in the Third Quarter taking a seven point lead with the successful point after kick.

Both Chris and Cory are directing and motivating their players. They are busy with other coaches to get input on their strategies.

The game progresses to the fourth quarter with neither team scoring. Lawson has the ball at the start of the fourth quarter and drives down the field, eventually scoring on a weary Smithville defense. The kick is good tying the game.

After Smithville is unable to get anything going on offense, Lawson begins a series of running plays eating up the clock. Chris is guiding his team down the field and Cory is unable to stop them. A couple of missed tackles and they score on a third down sweep from the twenty with three minutes to go in the fourth quarter, the kick is blocked. The scoreboard shows Smithville 13 Lawson 19 with less than three minutes left in the game.

Cory and Chris are looking across the field, pondering what the other can do to win the ball game. Both of them look determined and focused. Lawson kicks off and Smithville runs the ball back to the 40 yard line.

Chris and Cory are both getting more animated on the sidelines. Smithville runs the ball on an inside reverse to the Lawson twenty-nine yard line. The scoreboard clock says 1:24 left in the game. The announcer says "I would like to be at Sunday dinner at Momma Wohlford's this weekend. These boys have been battling since they were in diapers. This is nothing new to them, although we get a great seat to watch this one."

With just thirty-five seconds left, the Smithville Warriors need a magic play to win. Cory leans back in his chair with a sly look of confidence as he calls "135 zip blast...flea-flicker pass."

Chris is frantically trying to get the attention of his defensive backs and line-backers. "Prevent Defense!!! Stay back. Don't bite on the running play. Play it safe" Chris is yelling out on to the field to his players.

The pace is rapid as Smithville lines up. Chris is still yelling when the ball is snapped. The Quarterback comes down the line and it appears that Smithville is running the inside trap again. The Lawson players are drawn into the play, seeing the slot back get the ball on the inside reverse. At just the last moment before tucking into the line, he tosses the ball back to the quarterback. Streaking alone down the right sideline is senior wide receiver Doug Klusman. The quarterback drops back a step and launches a high arching pass that is caught over Klusman's shoulder as he crosses the end zone line for a touchdown. The Smithville crowd erupts in a loud cheer. As the teams line up for the extra point, the crowd is chanting the tomahawk chop.

Chris is bent at the waist with his hands on his knees. He stands tall and looks at the players, then looks over to his brother Cory sitting on the Pedestal. He laughs under his breath, knowing he has been had. He turns and looks at the big green scoreboard which reads Smithville 19 - Lawson 19 with no time on the clock.

The announcer gives the final play over the airwaves "Now the score is tied and the game rides on this kick. Smithville lines up to kick the extra point. It's good! What a finish as Smithville comes from six down to win with no time left on the clock."

The Smithville Coaches go to the pedestal and lower Cory. Both Coaching staffs meet at mid-field. The announcer continues "We have watched a dual of players and coaches here tonight. This was a beautiful high school football game. Congratulations to both teams."

Chris comes directly over to Cory. The grimace on his face shows he is not happy. It transforms into a feeling of admiration for his brother. "I can't believe you got away with that."

"I saw you trying to get your backs deep. I knew we had you then," says Cory

"I tried. You set us up. We called a *prevent*, but you got to the line too fast and we didn't get there."

The team is celebrating the victory and Cory is rolling off of the field with Chris walking beside him.

"Do you want to come over for a while and gloat? The coaches are coming to my house."

The other Lawson and Smithville coaches are heartily congratulating Cory.

"No. I have a few things to do. My own little celebration."

Chris perks up and teases his brother

"You be careful with that on-line stuff. Some gal may take advantage of you."

Cory responds "I could only wish. See you later."

They can't tell how tired he is and how he needed to get rest. Cory stops and looks up at his tall muscular brother.

"That was one heck of a coaching job tonight. Great job brother" says Chris.

Cory replies "Thanks" and rolls toward Jon and Becky who are standing on the sideline next to the pedestal. They are proud of their boys and their coaching tonight. Both have seen the sibling rivalry played out many times in the yard at home but this is one for the book. The newspaper clipping went into another scrap book that will eventually join her others in what she calls the family treasury. Together they go up the hill and leave the stadium. Cory is the victor, along with Big Jon and Becky his biggest fans.

CHAPTER 35

April Nights

Cory's bedroom, what used to be the parlor, is a large room in the center of the house. His bed is pushed against the wall which is covered with team and family pictures, trophies, and memorabilia from his playing and coaching days. Up in the corner is a large picture of him as a Coach at William Jewell. He is surrounded by the rest of the coaching staff, all dressed in Cardinal Red. Next to it is the first year coaching staff at Smithville. There are pictures of him making tackles in his Cardinal Red and team pictures of his high school and college teams. A couple of pictures stand out. One is Cory hitting a home run out of Royals Stadium in the All Star game the year before his accident. Another is when he put a hard hit on an opponent in college, upending him and causing a fumble. Another is of all three boys framed with the State Football Championship trophy between them. One of the most treasured pictures in the Wohlford family is a black and white copy of a Plattsburg Leader picture showing Cory and Chris holding footballs, basketballs, and gloves. They are two dominating young athletes with bright futures ahead of them.

On the other side of the room is Cory's work station. He has a large screen monitor and a powerful PC connected to the Internet. He is able to sit in his chair and communicate with the world. He has fashioned a special finger that resembles the Droid. Strapped to his hand, he can quickly type responses and correspondence with his many friends around the world. To them he is just another guy with a great sense of humor and wonderful outlook on life.

Over the years he has become more and more sophisticated with his technology and knows his ways around the social networks. Unless they have met him personally, they would never be able to tell that he has any disabilities. That is the way he prefers it. Although he is looking for a "special friend" that he can share his life with.

Most of us would jump at the chance to live in such a beautiful place with the trees and fields, the wildlife and lake. Cory loves it there but when the cold winter blows a snow or ice storm in, it could be weeks or months before it is safe for him to leave home. Just the trip down the ramp could be dangerous if it is covered with ice. He has had plenty of time to master his computer skills. What takes most of us a few minutes to write, it takes Cory much longer. He is OK with that, because it gives him the time to think about each word.

He has just returned home from coaching against Chris in the Smithville vs. Lawson game. A lamp is dimly lighting the area around his desk. His computer monitor is lit up illuminating his face as he is pecking out an E-Mail with a smile. He types "April, are we still on for Pizza Hut tomorrow at Noon? I am really looking forward to meeting you." Cory hits the send key and pulls himself up in his chair. A few seconds pass and the response beep is heard. Cory looks at the reply. "Great" he thinks then types "It's on 169 Highway in Smithville at Noon. See you then" Cory hits the enter key.

Before he turns off his computer for the night, he wants to send a note to his high school friend in North Carolina. He had gotten her email from a friend and they had been sending emails back and forth since then. Her latest email had come in the middle of a winter storm. She complained about the storm they were having in North Carolina and how it was so bad with major property damage. She sent him a picture of her deck. On it was a single lawn chair blown over. He laughed and remembered her beautiful blue eyes. Cory looked out the window at the full moon shining off two foot of snow. He typed his message to her about his upcoming date, then turns away from the computer.

It is a cool winter night in North Carolina. The silver bracelet no longer dangles from her wrist. She sees his email and eagerly reads it. She smiles with a warm heart.

Jon is sitting in a chair, visible in the next room. "Dad, can you help me get into bed please." Cory rolls over to the edge of the bed. Big Jon looks older now, but his shoulders are still broad and strong. He lightly and delicately lifts Cory and places him in bed, arranging and pulling the covers up around him.

"You sure coached a great game tonight. Chris didn't see that flea flicker coming."

"I told him I had some trick plays for him. Besides, he called the right defense but his players just bit on the fake into the middle" says Cory.

"We'll probably be hearing about that one for a while."

"Oh yeah, it was a good day all around Dad. I have a date tomorrow." Jon stands up and puts his hands on his hips looking down at Cory with a slight bit of concern. "Who?"

"Just a girl I met on line. We have been writing back and forth for a couple of months" replies Cory.

"She know about your chair?" Jon asks.

"Yes. Doesn't matter to her."

Jon lightens up and a smile comes across his face. "Sounds great to me. Good night."

Cory turns his head toward his Dad. "Thanks Dad. You've been great. Thanks for being here for me."

"Thank you. I wouldn't have it any other way. I am proud of you."

Jon reaches down and grabs Cory's hand with the Champion's grip, then lowers and kisses him on the cheek before turning off the lamp.

The next day is a big one for Cory. The pictures of April show a beautiful young woman. He can hardly wait to meet her. He awoke early and Jon helps him get up and going. After he has shaved, Jon brings in a splash of cologne that Becky really likes. Then they send him off in the van to meet April.

April sees Cory pull up in his van, watches the automatic doors swing open and the lift lowers him to the ground. She is standing at the door of the Pizza Hut, a short attractive blonde. Cory's contagious smile lights her up. They are both nervous.

Soon they are talking like old friends. Having spent six months in on-line conversations and telephone calls, they already know each other quite well. They eat and laugh and eat some more. Cory is really smitten by her beauty, charm, and wits. She in turn is impressed with his ability to overcome obstacles and his quickness to laugh. They have a great time and agree to meet again. She gives him a hug and kiss in the parking lot as he leaves his first date in ten years.

Six months later they are seeing each other on a regular basis. She is comfortable and at home with Cory. They are watching a movie on TV. April is sitting in a chair beside him and holding his hand. A funny love card is sitting on Cory's lap table. Cory is smiling widely and laughing at the movie. He turns to April and says, "Thanks again for the card. It is cute. Half a year and I forgot. I'm such a dunce."

"I can't believe it's been that long" She says.

"It's been a great time. Who would think that I would meet a beautiful blonde that I see eye to eye with."

They laugh and April rises up and kisses Cory. They hear the back door open, disrupting their kiss. Jon and Becky enter the room. Jon coughs. They both look exhausted.

"Glad your home. April brought up a couple of movies. What took you so long? Did you get in to see the doctor?"

Jon coughs a little harder this time. "Did they give you something for the cough?" he asks with concern.

Jon sits down hard on the couch, continuing to cough. Becky puts her purse down, sits down on the couch holding Jon's hand.

"He gave your Dad a prescription for oxygen and he is supposed to keep calm."

Cory responds "That should help you breathe better."

Jon leans to one side, trying to open his lungs, a grimace on his face.

"Damn Cancer" he says to himself.

Cory is sad to see his father in such pain. Big Jon has been there for him all his life whether it was taking him to baseball practice and games as boy, teaching him to throw in the yard or lifting him from his bed, dressing him and putting him in his wheelchair, he was always there.

"Is there anything else they can do?" asks Cory with frustration.

"Nothing" replies Becky softly.

Cory is stunned by the news. "Surely there is an operation or radiation or something?"

"I am going back to the specialist on Monday. He is going to have some test results." Jon coughs as he finishes his sentence.

A look of concern crosses Jon's face as he sees his son sitting in a wheel chair and knowing that it will be extra hard on Becky taking care of both of them. How can she handle being his only care provider when he dies?

"I am going to bed. I need a good night's sleep." Jon gets up and slowly goes to the bedroom.

"I need some sleep too. Can you help put me to bed April?"

Cory turns his chair with April and Becky following. After a few adjustments, together they use the lift that raises the big man from his chair and gently lowers him to his bed. Becky kisses Cory on the forehead and starts to leave.

"Mom, we're going to be all right." Becky stops with her arms crossed and looks back at Cory on the bed.

"It's terminal Cory. He has a lot of suffering to do yet." She pauses, reaches down, and grabs his hand with the champion's grip of his father. She places a light kiss on his cheek. "We've been through a lot together and we'll get through this too."

Becky leaves as April slides in beside Cory, resting her head on his shoulder. "Can you stay with me tonight?" April raises to an elbow where she can look into Cory's eyes. "I have to work tomorrow."

"I just need someone here. I'm scared about Dad." Cory is clenching his jaw and his eyes are darting back and forth. He feels like he is once again pinned in the car and there is nothing he can do for his Dad.

"I'll stay till you go to sleep." She assures him.

"That may be all night" he says. April adjusts herself and pulls the blanket up around him. Cory is staring at the ceiling, eyes wide open, anxiety on his face.

"What do you do when you're not sleeping?" she asks trying to calm him.

His face tightens as he thinks about the answer to her question.

"I talk to God. Pray for strength and pray for Mom and Dad. I also pray for all those people that have helped me over the years."

"You had better pray for your Dad now" She insists.

"I am" is all he can say.

CHAPTER 36

Goodbye Big Jon

Cory is living through a bitter sweet time. He had long ago accepted his disability and worked to minimize its effect on his life. He had found love from a beautiful woman. April and Cory had been together for nearly a year and things are going great with their romance.

Jon had gotten progressively worse as the cancer starts to take its toll on the big man. His last visit to the Doctor landed him in the hospital. His breathing is labored and energy sapped. He had started to feel worse when Cory visited him the next day. The pain had increased. All the years of smoking had taken its toll and Cory realizes it won't be long before his father is gone.

Becky is at the hospital in the early evening. April had come up to the home place. She and Cory are laughing and talking as she cleared the table and washed the dishes from the dinner she had cooked for him. The phone rings. April picks it up. "Hello. Hi Becky, we just finished dinner. Are you still at the hospital? I saved you a plate."

A sharp pain grabs her face and grows as she listens to Becky softly say "I'm afraid Jon is getting worse. The Doctor said that everyone should come down tomorrow, he probably won't last much longer."

April drops back into a chair at the table, puts her elbows on the table and tries to think of what to say to the strong and loving woman that might soothe her pain. "Oh my gosh Becky. I am so sorry" is all she could say as the sorrow rained down around her.

Cory adjusts himself and anxiously awaits the news he knows is coming. He sees the pain on April's face and recognizes the awful feeling in his gut, knowing that the news he is about to receive brings another change to their lives.

"What is it?" he asks. April can't speak as she hands the phone to Cory and starts to cry. "Mom, what's wrong?" Cory softly asks as he cradles the phone to his head.

Her voice is barely audible "He doesn't have long Cory. Can you call Steve and Chris? The Doctor thinks he may not live through the weekend."

The pain turns to steel resolve as Cory realizes he is about to be tested again. He must face this tragedy with the same resolve that has always been a part of his will. He knows he must lighten the load of his Mother or risk losing them both. "I'll take care of things here. I love you Mom" he says with tough resolve. He hears her soft goodbye and replies "Tell Dad I love him. He's my champion."

Cory puts the phone down and spins his chair around. April comes to him and holds him tight. He softy cries as she comforts him in her arms. His mind is racing, thinking of all of the things that he must do to help his mother as she endures the pain of losing her loving husband. He stiffens. "I have to call Steve and Chris."

He holds the phone with the hook in his hand and pushes the buttons with his tongue. He tenderly tells his brothers of the impending death of their father and asks them to join him at Big Jon's bedside.

Within twenty-four hours Steve had flown in from Indiana. He and Chris spend most of the day sitting with Big Jon. Jon is in bed breathing through an oxygen mask. Becky is standing next to him, Cory in his chair beside him. Steve and Chris are standing on the other side of the bed. They are talking of the good days before Cory's accident. Big Jon knows he doesn't have long. The room is filled with love and the memories of their lifetime together. Each one is grateful for the man who they love so dearly. Time slows down as the everyday worries and trivial problems in their lives fade away. Cory feels the grace of God and his warm hands wrap around his heart.

"Chris and I were just talking about how before my accident we were really flying high. Do you remember that double-header down at William Jewell? I think it was against Central Methodist? Chris hit home runs in both games and I pitched the saves in both games."

Jon slowly raises his hand as he weakly smiles behind the mask. Cory reaches out and Jon takes his hand with the Championship grip. Chris and Steve lightly take his other hand.

"And remember when we won the state championship in football" Chris says, flashing back to the field below the Arch in St. Louis.

"And Chris tore up his ankle, but still played in the second half. Remember when we got home and how black and blue Cory was?" added Steve.

"Three goal line stands" Chris proudly remembers.

"I remember the time that we beat Smithville in Basketball. Chris had eighteen points and I had thirty four" Cory softly recalls.

Becky reaches up and adjusts his oxygen mask. Slowly he speaks only getting out two words with every breath.

"You boys... Are the... Best sons ...a man could... Ever have. Take care... of Momma."

By now everyone is in tears. Jon can no longer speak and now only looks at his sons. They all feel him slipping away and are comforted knowing his faith sustains his soul and soon heaven will be his. Becky straightens his hair and caresses his face as he slowly closes his weary eyes for the last time.

CHAPTER 37

Shoes

The First Christian Church of Smithville is a large red brick church in downtown. The sanctuary has been a joyous place where they baptized their children, went to weddings, spent their holidays, and celebrated the lives of the ones they lost. Tonight the church is packed with friends wanting to say goodbye to a good friend. They milled in and out talking about Big Jon and the family. Each shared a story or two about Jon with each other.

Jon's casket is in the front of the church. A long line of friends and family are waiting to circle by and pay their last respects. Becky, the boys and their families are in the parlor at the rear of the church receiving the line after passing by the casket.

Coach Freeman waits patiently to the side. Finally a moment comes where he is able to step in line. He stops and looks at each of them. "Boys, you know I love you all. Your Daddy was like a brother to me. I was lucky to call him a friend. Thank you Becky for raising such a great family."

"Thank you Jim. You were always a favorite of Jon. You taught our boys more than football or track."

Jim hugs each one of the boys. When he gets to Cory he leans close and whispers in his ear "Your Daddy was the best." Coach stands and like so many years ago in the locker rooms he speaks so that everyone could hear, "Jon never let a kid go without athletic shoes. I thought it was just the Plattsburg kids he took care of. Every year we would have a few kids that needed help. The shoes always showed up as if out of thin air. The boys and girls never knew where they came from and Big Jon swore me to secrecy. In the years since, his legend lives on. You will never know how many coaches have told me that Big Jon also swore them to secrecy. He paid for hundreds of pairs of shoes over the years."

Becky is smiling next to Cory. Her memories of Big Jon's good deeds and his caring heart lighten her sorrow. Although her husband, her best friend has been called home, she takes comfort in knowing that his generous acts of kindness were beneficial to so many young people. It gives her strength.

During the next several months stories like this surfaced about Big Jon.

In Missouri a letter jacket is the ultimate honor for a boy in high school sports. A boy in one of the schools Big Jon sold sporting goods to had his letter jacket stolen. The green felt and leather sleeved jacket is his treasured possession. Having lettered as a freshman, his jacket was full of medals, All Conference, All District, All State and All Metro patches. Going into his senior year, he was recognized as a High School All American. He could only scrape enough money together to get the jacket. All his patches, medals and the big letter on the left breast are now gone and too expensive for him to replace. Big Jon had his own ideas when he ordered the jacket.

The jacket was delayed in arriving. School had started and the football season was underway. The boy waited patiently, and every time he saw Big Jon, he asked about the jacket. Then one day the boy was called to the Coaches office. Big Jon and the Head Football Coach walked in. Big Jon had the jacket in a nice garment bag. He took it out and the boy tried it on. It fit perfect and the boy was excited about being able to wear it to the game that night. Big Jon made him turn around and around before saying the jacket was too small. He made him make a few more turns and said that he will need to take it back and get one that was bigger. The boy took it off and with a sad heart, handed it back to the big man. Jon put it away then reached into the garment bag and pulled another jacket out. It had the same green felt and leather as the other. Jon handed it to the boy. "I know this one fits and you have to swear that you will never tell a soul where you got it" was all he said. Jon had all the patches re-made and sewn onto the jacket. The boy looked at the patches in disbelief. They were all showing consecutive years, including the present. "Now you know what is expected of you," said the Coach. It was then that the boy saw the High School All American patch, a white football trimmed in gold.

The next Friday night that young man's football team played the Plattsburg Tigers. It was still a couple of years before Big Jon's boys were starters for the Tigers. The boy scored a touchdown late in the game to lead his team to victory. Big Jon was standing on the sideline shaking his head as the boy jogged off the field. When their eyes met, they both laughed. Nothing more was ever said until they had coffee nearly thirty years later.

Lathrop High School is the closest rival to Plattsburg. Their school districts abut. Their rivalry goes back to the beginnings of their schools. One of their top athletes was Brian Bullock, who had played football against Chris and Cory. Brian tells the following story about Big Jon in an email to Cory.

"I was throwing the discus, warming up and really getting it out there. I remember like it was yesterday because I was really throwing well and my shot put was also really good. Somehow, on one of my practice throws I got a little too far on the last step and came down on edge of discus ring. I blew my ankle out and it immediately swelled up like a balloon. I don't know if you remember, but my Dad died April 2, 1981. I was feeling pretty low walking around the track and trying to 'walk out' the sprained ankle, which didn't really work. Big Jon, your Dad, came up and walked with me. He put his arm around me as we kept walking; he told me how sorry he was about my Dad. I will take that memory to my grave. Your dad was always about the kids and athletes. Yeah, he wanted his boys to win, as all parents do, but he also cared about all the kids, not just his own, and not just Plattsburg kids. Such a great memory. I will remember it for as long as I live."

Big Jon smiles.

CHAPTER 38

Tears

They are finally getting their rhythm that spring at the farm house that looked out over Smithville Lake. Jon's death in the fall had taken its toll on both Becky and Cory and now with the growing flowers they are once again clipping along.

Without even a blink, Becky had taken on all the tasks of caring for Cory, except when April comes to visit. It gives her a break. April was so good with Cory. Cory loves her and thoroughly enjoys their time together. Becky appreciates the time that April is there. It cheers Cory up and gives Becky time to do things for herself.

The dining room lights are off, with candles glowing on the table. A car door slams and the back door opens. Cory is sitting at the table which is set for two, a big smile on his face. April enters the dining room and puts her purse down.

"What is this Mr. Wohlford?"

"Just a romantic dinner for two."

Becky helped him set it up. Cory wanted something special for their first Valentine's Day.

"It is very beautiful Cory."

"Mom helped me. She's in the kitchen."

April crosses the room and gives Cory a big kiss.

"She is so wonderful. Oh Cory, this is so romantic"

She sits across Cory's lap and drapes her arms around his neck, looking deep into his eyes.

"You are the greatest."

"Then will you be my Valentine?"

"Of course I will, will you be mine?" she replied as she gives him another kiss.

"I'll take all of those I can get."

Several months go by and Cory is in bed late at night with the phone next to his head. He is talking with April. A picture of the two of them together sits on the nightstand. Cory remembers the events of their Valentine dinner.

"Valentines was a wonderful night. I feel so good when I am with you."

There is a long pause. Cory turns his head and adjusts the phone on the pillow. "I can't believe Dad has been gone five months either. He thought you were the greatest. I missed you last weekend. Are you coming up this weekend?"

There is another long pause. Cory's eyes are darting back and forth as if he is anticipating the answer.

"Cory. I am so sorry. I won't be up this weekend." Slowly and softly she says "Cory, I don't want to hurt you. I don't know how to tell you but I just can't handle it anymore. We live so far apart and I have my family to think about."

A look of sorrow washes over his face. They had been so happy together and now he knew by the sorrowful tone in her voice that their romance is quickly coming to an end.

"What? What do you mean?"

"I can't, I mean I am unable to handle it anymore. I love you but I can't do this anymore. I have a hard enough time taking care of myself."

"But I thought we had something special. You know I love you," grasping for anything to change her mind.

"I know Cory. I am just not strong enough to fully love you. We always said that we'd be honest with each other. It is not fair to you that I am unable to commit to us." The painful words are met with a sorrowful pause. "I am so sorry Cory. I have to go now. Good bye."

"Please, we can keep trying. I'll do anything to keep you." "I am so sorry. I don't want to hurt you, but I can't keep this up.

Believe me that this is tearing me up inside, I am sorry Cory. I have to go. Good bye."

Cory hears the dial tone so hangs up the phone. Pain is coursing through his heart. Becky is standing in the doorway, knowing as a mother that something is wrong. "What's wrong?" she softly asks even though her mother's instinct already knows. "April said she can't do this anymore...she can't handle this." With her heart as heavy as lead she reaches down and hugs her oldest son. Tears wet his pillow as he lay there unable to move and too tired to sleep.

CHAPTER 39

Pastor Witt

It is Sunday morning and Jo Ellen Witt, a pastor, is standing at the podium looking out over the crowded church. She is nearing the end of her sermon.

"Last year I attended the funeral of the husband of a friend of mine, Becky. When I walked into the church, I scanned the growing crowd for Becky and her sons. I spotted Cory, the first time I had seen him in many years - in his power wheelchair - and I saw Cory's twin, Chris with his family. Chris is a tall strapping 39 year old man who is the perfect picture of an athlete- still strong and robust. Cory on the other hand, is thin and unable to hold himself erect because he is paralyzed from the shoulders down. Cory was as strong as Chris as a child, youth and young adult. In fact, scouts from professional baseball teams were looking at him. However, at the age of 21, Cory was in a car accident and broke his neck. His strength is no longer in his body but in his soul."

Cory is sitting near the front of the church. People are sneaking glances at him.

She continues "I sent Cory an e-mail this week, telling him of my admiration for him and asking him to share the turnaround he has experienced in his life since his accident. Here are his words. 'The strength I have is from the way my parents brought me up with their values, my faith in the Lord, the peace I have within me and believe it or not, the playing of athletics. After my accident there were only two ways to go. Just hate the world for the rest of my life or deal with it. I still have my moments. Because of a great family and friends, I chose to deal with it.' The pastor pauses and looks around the room. Everyone is feeling uplifted. 'Finishing college, getting my degree then coaching were key factors. I think the drive, dedication, never giving up and trying to do things to my fullest one hundred percent of the time are things I got from athletic competition. Knowing that people still believe in me and treat me as a person helps."

The pastor pauses again, looking around the room, then with both hands on the podium she raises her voice.

"These are words from a strong man - strong in God's eyes and strong in my eyes. Let us pray."

The congregation bows their heads.

"God, we vacillate between confidence and pride and weakness and insecurity. Help us to realize who we are. Thank you for bringing Cory to us as an example to minister to us, helping us recognize your strength and carrying us where you want us to be. Amen."

The congregation files slowly out of the church, many of them stopping and grasping Cory's shoulder or offering a kind word. Cory is smiling and strong.

CHAPTER 40

Answered Prayers

She sat at her kitchen table wondering what was next for her life. She left her hometown nearly thirty years earlier to go to college, with definite plans for her future. Her goals were lofty and a girl with her gumption had the tools to make things happen. She was smart, good looking, athletic and had an inner drive that was infectious as she headed to the University of Missouri to continue her education.

Tonight she had to make some decisions. She loved her friends and the place she lived. She thought this was too big for her, so she turned it over to God and at that table in the early evening hours she prayed for healing and direction in her life.

Two decades earlier she left Mizzou for St. Louis with a degree under her arm and a dream in her heart. Everyone she met could see the spark in her eyes as she touched many people's hearts. Growing up on a farm, she knew the value of hard work and enjoyed its rewards.

Unfortunately, a bad marriage ended and now she had to re-evaluate what was important to her. Over the years she had moved to Kentucky and North Carolina always keeping in touch with her friends back home. As she took stock in her life she thought about all the people she loved and all the people she could trust. Her mind kept coming back to the down-to-earth people she had grown up with and the love of her family. She knew in her heart that it was time to go home.

She grew up on a scenic farm, still worked by her parents. She always knew that she could go home and now as her parents aged, going home was the right thing to do. Leaving friends in North

Carolina was tough. Her emotions are still raw from the marriage. The best prescription for her was a good dose of family. Like a warm blanket it provided a place to heal her heart and start life anew in her hometown of Plattsburg, Missouri.

Her parents welcomed her with arms wide open. Their beautiful daughter had returned and brought a new life to the farm. She enjoyed getting back into the routine she left so many years before. Planting a garden, sewing everything from curtains to dresses for the Nuns going to convent, working the fields and barn. For nearly a year she healed.

Cory kept alive his search for a special friend to share his love. His social networking gave him further hope that he will one day find that love.

Along came Holly Starr. She knew Cory from her student days at Smithville High School and they later connected on the Internet. She admired him for his courage and the inspiration he gave to everyone around him. They became friends and like little kids they teased each other. She knew his dream and wanted to help Cory find the special friend he was praying for. A celebrity spokesperson in the Kansas City television market, she has lots of fans and Cory is one of her biggest.

Holly is well versed on social media. Her Facebook friends number in the thousands. She is smart and quick witted so she and Cory get along quite well. She and Jennifer, her mother, encouraged Cory to get a Facebook page so that old and new friends could find him and maybe he could meet a special friend through them. When he finally signed up, something magical happened.

Life in Plattsburg has not changed much since her youth and was certainly different than North Carolina. A quick drive through town revealed a few changes, but for the most part, things are pretty much the same as she left them. Her friends are older now. Some of them married young, others married multiple times. Getting caught up with everyone and re-establishing old relationships was fun.

As the year progressed, she was a substitute teacher at the schools in the area and loved being around the kids. She has applied at the schools in Plattsburg and Smithville, but her timing was off and their needs didn't match up.

On a warm summer evening in the summer of 2009 she was sorting through the boxes yet unpacked from her move. On the side of one box was written "photo albums." Her heart jumped. She loved to do scrap books and the box contained the treasures of her life. Picking it up, she hurried up from the basement and landed in the middle of the living room floor.

The box was heavy and her anticipation high as she opened it. Out she pulled several decorated albums. Looking at the outside she could tell when they were assembled and had a good idea what they contained. The most recent are on top and she slowly turned the pages remembering the friends that she left behind. She was still able to keep in touch with calls, letters, and most recently her new Facebook page. The evening ended with her dozing on the couch, memories running through her head.

The next morning she awoke to find her memories stacked on the coffee table. She made it halfway through the box, cherishing each page. Her Mom passed by the door and decided to get some of her family albums out also. Soon they are laughing and crying remembering all of the good times and the loved ones.

Turning the pages they came upon an old newspaper article she had saved. There stood Chris and Cory holding a football, basketball and baseball bats. She fondly remembered the Wohlford boys. She had been close to them in high school. Turning the page she remembered that Cory had been injured in a horrible car accident. She had sent him an email from North Carolina a few years earlier after seeing that the Kansas City area had been blanketed by a cold winter storm. She titled it "Severe Storm Damage in North Carolina." When he opened the attachment it showed a lawn chair blown over on her deck.

Soon the albums were put down and they are outside picking and breaking green beans from the garden. Since it is the first week of

July, a few tomatoes had come on and they would be good with a mess of beans. She asked her Mom if she knew what Cory was doing now. "I believe he is still coaching football at Smithville."

The boxes and albums got pushed to the side as they celebrated Independence Day. She sees so many people in town and is able to get caught up quickly with her old high school girlfriends. She recognizes several of the players from the State Champion Football team of 1979. Memories came roaring back to her with the faces and names.

She had been a cheerleader, played basketball and ran track. More suited for the wood shop, she preferred to be around the guys because she knew she could fix almost anything broken on the farm and loved showing them how. She loved cheering the football team to victory and had a real competitive streak in her when playing basketball and running track.

That night when she got home she pulled out her yearbooks from high school. Flipping through the pages she started to recall the games, track meets, and parties from her youth. The black and white photos of smiling kids, ready to take on life. When she got to the track page it all came rushing back to her. She and the Wohlford twins were at one time the best of friends. They rode together on the bus to the meets. When they were together, they laughed a lot and won a lot of track medals.

She thought back to a cold winter night after a basketball game during her senior year. She invited a bunch of kids to her parents' house, including the newly licensed twins. It had been spitting snow when they left the school and by the time they arrived, the snow was blowing hard. The group was having so much fun, they didn't care. Soon after midnight, Cory finally called Big Jon who knew where they were. He told them to spend the night and get home when the snowplows came through in the morning. She smiled as the memory filled her heart. She was amazed at how much they ate for breakfast the next morning.

The Fourth of July celebration had come and gone. Sweet corn is ready in the garden. She had plenty to do around the farm. Up in the morning, she is picking beans and shucking corn. After lunch they pull some weeds and mow the yard when needed. It was all good work and left her tired and happy at night.

Once again she pulled the box out from the corner in the living room where she had left it the week before. She had only gone halfway down into the box. Dumping the whole stack of scrap books out of the box, she heard a clink on the table. Moving the albums out of the way, she saw the bracelet and her heart jumped. She had forgotten about it. At one time it was her most prized possession. It was given to her for her eighteenth birthday. Picking it up from the table, she felt the weight of the silver. Her name was inscribed on the plate. It shined in the lamplight. Happiness filled her as she remembered the wonderful times with her friend Cory. Tears filled her eyes as she turned it over and saw the date inscribed on the back. That night she wore it to bed.

The next morning she awoke to a warm summer day. The bracelet was still on her wrist at breakfast. During the past year she stayed in touch with her friends in Kentucky and North Carolina by using Facebook. She wondered if Cory might be on Facebook. She would love to catch up with him. After breakfast, she sat down at her computer and pulled up her account. At the top of the page is a box where you can look up friends by typing in their names. How many Cory Wohlfords can there be? She typed in his name.

At the insistence of Holly, Cory finally gave in and signed up for a Facebook account. He is really getting a charge out of finding old friends. He would get a request and send a request. Holly was right and his social life took on a whole new dimension. On Facebook, he is able to see who a person really was by their writing. It didn't matter if they wore designer clothes or drove expensive cars. He enjoyed looking at their pictures and catching up with old friends.

Something happened one morning in early July. He is on the ESPN website when an alert hit his email. Down in the corner of the monitor is a message he had seen hundreds of times. It is a Facebook friend request. This message made his heart skip a beat. It simply read: Brenda Norton wants to be your friend on Facebook.

Since his accident, Cory has limited use of his hands. They are curled and he is unable to grasp small items. He is able to attach a single aluminum finger to type on his computer. It takes him a little longer than most to reply with his one key at a time pecking. Today it is like lightning. The smile on his face is so big that when Becky comes walking through the parlor with the mail, she has to ask, "What are you up to?" Cory just smiles and nods his head as Brenda Norton's Facebook wall is up on his screen. "Is that our Brenda? She is beautiful." Cory agreed on both counts. "She sent me a friend request" he says with a big smile.

Cory went to bed that night with a sore jaw. He had been on Facebook with Brenda getting caught up. They talked for two hours by phone and his smile could light a million candles. At dinner that night, he kept smiling. Before he went to bed he checked again just to see if he was dreaming. Her last post to him that night was "Good night Cory. We'll talk tomorrow. Love Brenda."

Cory didn't sleep much that night and neither did Brenda. Cory kept going back into his memories and playing them over and over always remembering something new. It was like a motion picture that kept rewinding. Every time it did, something new and wonderful was remembered.

Brenda lay in bed also remembering their youth. She is amazed that Cory had not changed. He is still smart, witty, quick, and charming. She looked forward to talking with him again. The last time she had any correspondence with him was a Thank You card she sent him for the present when she graduated from Mizzou in 1985. It had been there beside him, in the floorboard of the Blue Max.

The next morning Cory is waiting anxiously at his computer. He was on Facebook looking up other people he remembered in the night. On several of their pages he saw her picture on the left side denoting that she is a friend. He couldn't wait to tell Holly. A simple note he wrote. "Found an old friend on Facebook. Stay tuned." Holly knew something was up with her friend and prayed that it was special.

Brenda had some errands to run in the morning. She had to go to Plattsburg for some pickling spice because she is going to pick and pickle some cucumbers in the afternoon. She went early so she could get back and see if Cory was on Facebook. Her anticipation surprised her. She had been asked out and gone on a few dates since returning to the farm, but this is different.

Putting the bags on the kitchen table she went directly to her computer and turned it on. Pulling up Facebook, she sees that he is in the Chat box so she immediately pulls him up. After a few more sessions, a long evening call that night and more the next day, Cory finally asks her out. She graciously accepts his offer.

They met for their date. He quietly noticed the silver bracelet on her wrist.

CHAPTER 41

The Next Team

Smithville has one of the best football facilities in the state. During Cory's twenty plus years coaching, they have achieved success winning Conference and District Championships. The support of the community is evident with the large crowds and strong support of the Warriors. One goal still stands, win a State Championship.

The team is filing onto the field before practice. It is near the middle of the season. The Coaches follow Cory as he rolls onto the field. Becky knows there is going to be a special announcement and has come to Warrior Stadium. She is listening near the concession stand and out of the view of the players.

Coach Greg Smith gathers the players around him. "Ok, everybody up." The team takes a knee. All are looking up at Coach Smith. "Before we get started, there is one very important thing that each of you should know. Today we begin another drive to a District Championship. I have heard some great news to kick it off. Among us is a true Champion. The school was notified that Coach Wohlford was nominated and is one of the finalists for a prestigious National Coach of the Year Award."

The boys erupt into loud cheers, proud of the man they all admire and call Coach. They know first-hand of his dedication. Several of them went to the website and nominated him. The stories they wrote about him had gotten the attention of the nominating committee. The website asks; Is your Coach at the top of their game? Does your Coach stand out? One of the boys responded, "My Coach stands heads and shoulders above us all, from the seat of his wheelchair for the past twenty-three years."

Throughout the years he has been recognized for his coaching ability. He coaches from the heart giving his all, just to be on the field with the boys. Through the blazing heat of the summer training camps to the cold winter Friday night lights and all of the grinding practices between, Coach Wohlford is there. When asked "Why do you dedicate yourself to these boys year after year?" He humbly replies "If my circumstances or actions can positively influence one of these players, he may go on to be a great man of faith. Just one is worth it." He has coached hundreds if not thousands of young men who today still recall the inspiration he gave them to persevere in the face of all odds and never surrender.

The team runs onto the football field as Cory and the coaches follow. They continue to work toward another Championship season.

Becky, a proud and strong mother, is walking away and up the hill. Because of her never ending love and care she provides her child, she is a hero to many. She reaches out her hand and a beautiful blonde wearing a green Warrior pullover fleece joins her walking arm in arm up the hill. On her left wrist she wears her most prized possession.

THE BEGINNING

EPILOGUE

Jon and Becky started their young family and brought them up in a one hundred year old white two story farmhouse on a hundred acre farm that had been in Becky's family for over a hundred years. The home place sits on a ridge at the edge of the small village of Trimble, Missouri. From their front porch is a panoramic view of the rolling hills that surround Smithville Lake. These are farm fields that change throughout the year with every season. When you roll up into the driveway, the view is striking no matter what time of year you arrive. The lush green fields in the spring are followed by a hot summer sun that brings out the lighter colors before plunging into the reds and browns of the fall. The winter can be cold and desolate at times, but a frequent snow can change the ground into a winter wonder land with icicles hanging from the trees.

The land is rich with wild deer, raccoons, rabbits, squirrels, foxes, coyotes, and opossums. Birds migrate through the area including white Canadian geese, mallards, martins, cardinals, blue jays, and an abundance of hawks, eagles and falcons. Every farm has a garden. Orchards and vineyards dot the landscape. It is beautiful country. This is how the Wohlford's live, in a sanctuary filled with family and the company of their community. Because they love so deeply, they are so loved by their family, friends, and the community.

Their sons were brought up to be kind, considerate, and respectful. If they weren't, Jon had a way of dealing with them. They regularly attended Church and were involved in the community. There were no excuses in the Wohlford family. They never surrender.

Acknowledgements

God Bless you Becky Wohlford. You have enduring power and love. Thanks for sharing it.

Thanks to my wife and kids, Julie, Tyler, and Kari. Thanks Mom and Daddy Davidson, Cindy Green, Terry and Garry Davidson.

Thanks to my wonderful friends who read and critiqued this incredible story. You are always in my heart. Kristi Awad, Carla Harmon, Alison Payne, Bill Buckley, Chris Maxfield, Don Hanks, Elizabeth Anderson, Kevin Perz, Bob Beltz, Bob Haffeman, Shap Boyd, Bobby Dunn and Holly Starr.

Thank you Jackie Conrad for your gentle editing.

Special thanks to Coaches Jim Freeman, Vic Wallace, Bill Maas and all the great coaches Cory has worked with. You have been great team mates for our Champion.

Bless Denney Fales, Greg Summers, David Gipson and the many friends that have been there through thick and thin.

Thank you Chris and Steve Wohlford for your brotherly love and the rest of Cory's family for their love and support.

Brenda Norton – you are an answered prayer. May all your dreams come true.

Thank you Cory Wohlford for the inspiration, love, hope, encouragement, patience and showing us all how life can be lived to the fullest when you never surrender.

Bob Davidson lives at the beach
with his beautiful wife,
blonde soccer playing daughter,
BIG football playing son,
blue eyed dog,
leopard gecko,
a gator named Truman
and a cat that talks.

Made in the USA
Charleston, SC
17 January 2011